ALLAN MORRISON is a prolific author; his previous books include *Last Tram tae Auchenshuggle!* which combines three of his passions: humour, nostalgia and Glasgow. His media appearances include The One Show, Richard and Judy and The Fred MacAulay Show.

He is involved in charity work and after-dinner speaking, and is a member of his local Rotary club. Allan enjoys hill-walking, sport and travel, and is a keen football supporter. He and his wife live in the West of Scotland, and he is the proud grandfather of four grandchildren.

Should've Gone tae Specsavers, Ref!

ALLAN MORRISON

with illustrations by
BOB DEWAR

Luath Press Limited

EDINBURGH

www.luath.co.uk

First Published 2013

ISBN: 978-1-908373-73-1

The paper used in this book is recyclable. It is made
from low chlorine pulps produced in a low energy,
low emissions manner from renewable forests.

Printed and bound by
Martins the Printers, Berwick upon Tweed

Typeset in Sabon and MetaPlus by 3btype.com

Contents

Acknowledgements

For their encouragement, help and advice my thanks go to the staff at the Scottish Football Museum at Hampden, especially Blair James, the Visitor Support Officer. Also John Allan, Jim Crumlish, Eric and Val Grieve, Ron Hachey, Craig and Lorna Morrison, Andrew Pearson, Lynne Roper, Robert Russell, the late Ron Sheridan, Margaret Wallace, Archie Wilson, John and Morag Wilson.

Introduction

FOOTBALL IS THE PEOPLE'S GAME. People enjoy watching it almost as much as they enjoy playing it and fan culture is a vibrant and expressive aspect of football. Scotland's national obsession is an incurable disease, a collective insanity. Triumph, tragedy and heart-stopping excitement... that's Scottish football.

The game is a form of identity for many supporters, with clubs acting as a focal point in many a community. It is said that there are two things you can never change in life – your mother and your football team. Fan passion, agitation and noise add atmosphere and energise matches, so entertaining the crowd is fundamental. And supporters are most definitely their team's 12th man.

Scottish football has existed since time immemorial. Wild Scotsmen kicked around the heads of unfortunate Roman soldiers foolish enough to venture north, which resulted in dispatches being sent to Italy that the Romans might be better to avoid this dangerous place. Teams of Italian stonemasons were swiftly dispatched to the periphery of the Empire to build a wall under the watchful eye of Emperor Hadrian, who blatantly ignored planning permission in order to keep the Scottish footballing tribesmen away from the civilised south.

There are many recorded games of football played

at large festivals and gatherings throughout the years, though many of them would come under the category of 'mob football'. Early football matches appear to have been rough, indeed sometimes brutal, contests.

Although most games were portrayed as violent, there were clearly some with an element of skill. In 1568 such a game was witnessed by Mary Queen of Scots, during her imprisonment at Carlisle Castle. An account of the game states:

> Twenty of her retinue played at football before her for two hours, very strongly, nimbly, and skilfully, without foul play – the smallness of their ball occasioning their fairer play.

The reference to the size of the ball fits in with an amazing discovery made while renovation work was being done at Stirling Castle in the 1970s. High up in the roof beams of the Queen's Bedchamber a ball was discovered which has been dated as originating from between 1537 and 1542. It is reckoned to be the oldest existing football in the world.

The early part of the 19th century would witness the birth of the modern game. In 1824, John Hope, a student at Edinburgh University, founded the world's first football club. Apparently Hope created the 'Foot-Ball Club' in order that he and his friends could regularly play football.

The members of the Third Foot-Ball Club all paid subscription fees and John Hope kept a careful record of the club's accounts. These accounts refer to the purchase of 'hail-sticks' (goalposts), bladders and leather casings. Rules were also drawn up which included a rule banning tripping, and one whereby a free kick could be awarded when the ball went out of bounds. Unfortunately the Third Foot-Ball Club went out of existence in 1841, probably owing to John Hope and his friends getting a little old to play. In 1874 Hope was involved in creating Edinburgh's first Association club, the 'Third Edinburgh Rifle Volunteers FC'.

Football has been played in Scotland wherever there has been a reasonably flat open space. It could be 'tanner ba' street games (so called because a small rubber ball cost a sixpence, known colloquially as a tanner) or alternatively a bald tennis ball, a burst beach ball, a bundle of rags or newspapers all tied with string were used, although in the latter case when it rained, the ball would come apart. Stranger options used were wicker balls or sometimes even pigs' bladders. Open spaces gradually gave way to gravel and cinder pitches on which many a footballer ended up with skint knees. Mothers were continually complaining to their offspring about scuffed shoes and boots.

Football nowadays has an inviolate place in the Scottish national psyche. Scotland loves this game that, in just 90 minutes, can take you on an emotional rollercoaster. Then there's the charisma of great players, the passion of the fans, some of it served unfortunately with a spoonful of sectarianism. Players are at the heart of the game. Some are natural goal scorers, others great defenders, while others have all round skill and flair.

The famous Scottish 'Tartan Army' of supporting foot soldiers faithfully invades other countries, mixing with other teams' supporters in a friendly manner. And the Tartan Army stay faithful to the cause, regardless of the outcome of the battle.

Nowadays you can't have a football match without a referee, and although it is a tough job, it's their own choice that they cop an earful from thousands of people while having their eyesight and parentage called into question. Even the fourth official gets it in the neck, although you have to ask what purpose is served in haranguing a fellow when one of his jobs is merely holding up a board to show the numbers of substituted players or the amount of added time.

Someone once said:

> Every football team could use someone who knows how to play every position, knows when a player is definitely offside and knows when it's a penalty. The only problem is that it's difficult getting him to put down his pie and Bovril and come down from the terracing or stand.

That's why we need referees.

This book's hero, Big Erchie, first made his mark with the Scottish media and public when he red-carded all 22 players, plus the linesmen, in a Highland League match. Now, in the mainstream Scottish football arena of bigotry, booze and Bovril, Big Erchie tries to apply impartial judgement although his humour can be withering at times. And the poor man carries a terrible burden... he's a secret Partick Thistle supporter.

Meet Big Erchie

AN ARTICLE ON THE PRIORITIES OF LIFE talks about the need for food, clean water, oxygen and sleep as fundamental to living, plus some of the biological homeostatic mechanisms keeping us alive. It goes on to identify money and financial investments as being important. Amazingly, there is not one mention of the key essence of life dominating Scotland: football. Football, the life blood of Scotland with its key ingredients of closed minds, pies, Bovril and prejudice, a game with 22 players, two linesmen and tens of thousands of 'referees'.

Our hero, Big Erchie, was brought up on a farm in Perthshire, making him resilient to wind, rain, snow, mud, midges, ramblers, bawling bulls, bolshie coos and awkward critters. His father had once played football for Partick Thistle, and relics of a bygone age sat in a display cabinet in the farm living room, much to the chagrin of Erchie's mother. They consisted of an old leather lace-up football, a pump, an adaptor, an inner tube and some patches.

Bestride his father's throbbing old Massey Ferguson tractor, Erchie was master of all he saw, while on either side his two dedicated sheepdogs awaited his shrill whistle. Clearly this was a perfect finishing school for a life in football refereeing with his very own Field of Dreams, although Erchie sometimes commented that the dogs reacted quicker than some players. But no longer does Erchie live in a rural area. He has now stayed for many years in an apartment in the heartland of football bigotry: Glasgow.

Erchie's hooded, steely eyes – the cumulative effect of years peering through perpetual drizzle – his thin slash of a mouth, and his now well-known streak of thrawn ruthlessness have given him a commanding, no-nonsense look, much recognised by the media, the Scottish footballing fraternity, the Scottish Professional Football League (SFA), and anyone who has reached the argumentative stage of the inebriated in his local hostelry in Glasgow's city centre. Unfortunately, from time to time, Erchie's wicked sense of humour and wisecracks do get him into trouble.

Loved by the press as one of Scottish football's characters, Big Erchie has adapted his lifestyle to suit his persona. His tractor has given way to other trusty steeds. Once it was a Triumph motorbike because he had been impressed by Marlon Brando riding his in *The Wild One*. Nowadays it's a Harley Davidson Electra Guide Ultra Classic upon which he zooms in devil-may-care mode to each stadium with his black leathers, gauntlets, Arai helmet and trailing raffish scarf (carefully chosen for its neutral colours). He is no Hell's Angel, though many football fans think otherwise.

In the match officials' changing room along with his assistant referees, and the distinctive aroma of long forgotten football socks, jock-straps and sweaty shirts, his preparation is something to behold. After all, the match might be on the telly.

Standing his ground and insisting that a player come and talk to him after committing a foul can bring abject terror to the perpetrator of the misdemeanour. Suddenly players appear baffled, incredulous or apparently absentminded as to their alleged conduct. Although Erchie is well known for letting play flow to a team's advantage after an obvious foul, he surreptitiously watches the culprit for the rest of the time the player is on the park, which may not be overlong.

A booking by Big Erchie is a painstaking ritual for both player and referee as Erchie calmly and prosaically enters the name and number of the offender in his book with the care of a monk drawing an illustrated letter, while at the same time gutting and filleting the culprit using his wicked sense of humour in a voice reminiscent of an acetylene torch set on full heat. Alas, on occasion, a frustrating petulant demonstration of power causes him to show a red card when a yellow would probably have sufficed.

Deep in his bosom, Big Erchie is consumed by a loathing of 'simulation', especially such exhibitions as diving in the box or when a player is through on goal. 'Some of that lot should not only get a red card but Oscar nominations thrown in,' he continually moans. His trademark waving of his arms accompanied by a snort and roll of the eye suggests that, for some players, the rack, thumbscrew or the birch would not be inappropriate.

Life on the cutting edge of professional football is not easy, especially now that he is now no longer in the first flush of youth and is continually witnessing a parade of pimply referees who are yet to start shaving entering the footballing ranks. However Erchie, though smaller than most, is still reasonably fit, mobile, astute, never nonplussed, technically accomplished and utterly ruthless.

With senior teams in Scotland now employing large numbers of foreign players with a limited English vocabulary (although many of the Scottish players suffer from the same deficiency), Erchie has devised his very own style of hand waving and finger pointing much loved by press photographers.

Erchie has his favourite players past and present. Denis Law, Kenny Dalglish, Jim Leighton, Jimmy Johnstone, Brian Laudrup, Henrik Larsson, Willie Miller and Gaza (though Erchie always thought he was inclined to use his elbows over much) are just a few among his litany of icons. Indeed, talking about some of these individuals and their skills can make him moist-eyed, his heart palpitating. For Erchie always recognises talent but can also be appreciative of the player who, although lacking in natural ability and somewhat raw, gives it his best.

Our hero dislikes 'the establishment' in general, but appreciates that his employers at the SPFL specifically select him for games where his renowned discipline is necessary to ensure the game will not get out of hand.

Every match is different. For instance, Scottish local derbies can involve a gruesome, feral ritual of mayhem and bloodletting. Treacherous swamps, shark-infested waters, minefields and snipers' alleys can sometimes be preferable to meeting disgruntled fans with their effing and blinding after such sanguinary games.

Despite criticism, Erchie is never churlish or vindictive. He recognises that footballers came in a phalanx of shapes, sizes and temperaments. Sometimes he opts to be considerate of players' idiosyncrasies, merely chastising them surprisingly gently while ominously chuckling quietly to himself. He prefers players who readily acknowledge a situation and he absolutely abhors whingers.

His tolerance does not go as far as mistakes made by other referees when he is acting as an assistant referee. Then he can be heard shouting abuse at them into his mike, especially when they make decisions apparently plucked from the far flung corner of unlikelihood.

Being relatively small in stature (there is no minimum height restriction for referees) he can at times be almost spectral as he ghosts in and out of groups of players, stopping personal feuds and sorting out shoving and pushing at corner kicks.

His love of the 'beautiful game' is such that he takes a personal interest in the line-up formations of teams, sometimes being amazed at the starting eleven selected by managers. And to oversee his beloved soccer he is happy to not only turn out on sunny afternoons at large prestigious grounds, but also ash-grey stadia at the fag end of some unremarkable town in the depths of winter. As Erchie has remarked: 'Ah've even refereed at small grounds where, with their attendances, they announce the names of the spectators to the teams!'

Scottish weather can play a significant part in refereeing, with some games on a knife-edge as to whether or not they go ahead. Erchie's number one concern is wind, when his carefully combed hair can be impacted, leaving an exposed shining pate vulnerable to the lens of photographers. However he does admire the stoicism of players and fans who turn up for matches on a day when even dogs refuse to leave home.

Attention-grabbing headlines which praise his refereeing expertise are carefully preserved by Erchie in a series of albums. Any newspaper reviews which attack his quirkiness and independence of spirit are quickly dispensed with. He considers the opinions of Scottish sportswriters on the whole to be a mish-mash of bollocks and pig-headedness.

Big Erchie's self-esteem is sacrosanct to his overall image, and even his appellation as 'Big Erchie' instils pride, as it is acknowledged by all and sundry that he is somewhat special to the Scottish game. Stories proliferate as to his part in dauntingly difficult matches both in Scotland and elsewhere with his reputation for sorting out aggressive and violent behaviour. Lusty, unsophisticated chanting of his name from the terracing is music to his ears, and he hopes that his masters at the

SPFL listen to the acknowledgement of his expertise by the paying punters.

Big Erchie's idea of relaxation away from refereeing is to immerse himself in the music of Elgar, especially 'Enigma Variations' and 'Land of Hope and Glory'. Elgar had endeared himself to Big Erchie when he learned that the composer loved football and had supported Wolverhampton Wanderers.

Sometimes of a Saturday night, sipping his favourite malt whisky, Big Erchie sits and watches a match on the telly he has just refereed, cringing when the high profile scrutiny of up to 23 cameras capture a doubtful decision on his part.

Throughout the years he has borne abuse and verbal lacerations by Scottish fans of all teams without any bitterness, enduring the weekly jibes with dignity, secretly believing his judgement to be better than that of thousands of biased eejits.

And, regardless of the final score, Erchie always regards himself as the real star in every match.

Scotland's National Stadium

HAMPDEN PARK IS THE OLDEST continually used international stadium in the world. It has been on its present site in the Mount Florida area of Glasgow since it was first opened in October 1903.

The owner of Hampden Park is Queen's Park FC, nicknamed 'The Spiders'. The motto on their coat of arms is 'Ludere, Causa, Ludendi', translating as 'The Game for the Game's Sake'. The team play in the Scottish Professional Football League, although all players are amateurs.

Queen's Park FC is the oldest club in Scottish football still in existence. It dates back to 1867. They have played at a venue known as Hampden Park since 1873. It is interesting to note that the first Hampden Park was located near to a terrace named after a certain John Hampden, who apparently had fought for the Roundheads in the English Civil War.

Queen's Park FC played at the first Hampden Park from 1873 to 1884. The location is now a bowling club situated at the junction of Queen's Drive and Cathcart Road. The club then moved to its second home about 150 yards from the original after the Cathcart District Railway planned a new line through the site of the club's western terrace.

Twelve acres of land off Somerville Drive were acquired in 1899. Twin grandstands along the south side of the ground were built with a pavilion wedged between them. The surrounding natural slopes were then shaped to form banks of terracing.

Hampden Park was the biggest stadium in the world when it fully opened in 1903, but was surpassed by the Maracana Stadium in Rio de Janeiro, Brazil, in 1950. With Ibrox Stadium and Celtic Park as well, Glasgow possessed the three largest football stadia in the world in 1903.

The first match to be played at Hampden was on 31 October 1903 when Queen's Park defeated Celtic in the league. The first Scottish Cup Final played in the stadium was between Rangers and Celtic in 1904 with a record Scottish attendance at that time of 64,672.

The first Scotland versus England international match took place in 1906 with 102,741 fans in attendance. This match was to establish Hampden as the home of the Scottish team.

Attendances continued to rise with 121,452 attending the 1908 Scotland versus England game. The 1909 Scottish Cup Final between the Old Firm attracted 131,000 in total over the first match and replay. Unfortunately there was a riot at the end of the replay when the match again ended in a draw. The fans had demanded that the match should be played to a conclusion. It was decided to withhold the trophy as the playing surface wasn't deemed to be in a fit state for another replay. In response to this riot the Scottish Football Association decided for a time not to use

Hampden as a Cup Final venue. However, after WWI the stadium was again used for finals from 1920 onwards.

Queen's Park FC purchased extra land in 1923 bringing the total to some thirty-three and a half acres. As a result 25,000 places were added to the terraces. Rigid crush barriers were installed in 1927.

It was around this time that the phrase 'Hampden Roar' came into vogue. With the layout of the terracing and stands, and so many in attendance, the roar when Scotland scored a goal could be deafening. The 'Hampden Swirl', when wind could suddenly play havoc with the ball, was another unique phenomenon of the ground. Today's Hampden, with its much reduced attendances and new layout of the ground, does not provide the same effects.

Subsequent ground improvements increased the official capacity of Hampden to 183,388 but the SFA restricted the number of tickets to 150,000 for games to alleviate crushing.

During WW2, matches at large grounds were initially prohibited due to fear of bombing by the Luftwaffe. Scottish National League and Cup competitions were suspended for the duration of the conflict with limited regional and cup competitions established in their place. A government order was placed on Queen's Park FC stating that Hampden, and the smaller pitch nearby known as Lesser Hampden, be ploughed up and used for the growing of vegetables. The committee decided to ignore the order and, amazingly, government officials did not pursue the matter further.

On Christmas day 1945, a fire destroyed the stadium press box and damaged many offices. The press box was subsequently replaced with a two-storey structure which overhung the pitch.

In the Scottish Cup Final of 1948, played on 17 April, Rangers and Morton drew 1–1 after extra time. The attendance was 129,176. The replay took place on 21 April, Rangers winning 1–0 after extra time. The attendance was 133,750.

Arson was responsible for a fire in the south stand in October 1968, destroying 1,400 seats, one of the team dressing rooms and some offices. This caused the 1968–69 Scottish League Cup Final to be postponed until April.

By the 1970s it was obvious that Hampden was in need of significant renovation. Wembley Stadium had been revamped for the 1966 World Cup. Public safety issues were highlighted after the disaster at Ibrox in January 1971 when 66 fans were tragically crushed to death. The safety of Sports Grounds Act of 1975 compelled stadiums to be licensed and meet safety requirements. In addition, crowd segregation and restrictions on numbers were imposed. Ibrox and Pittodrie were duly converted to all-seater stadiums and Hampden's capacity reduced to 81,000.

Unfortunately, funding was a problem. Queen's Park FC had insufficient funds and Glasgow District Council withdrew its funding, and at that time the Government also opted not to support renovation.

However in 1992, the UK Government eventually provided a grant of £3.5 million which allowed work to begin on converting Hampden into an all-seater stadium. Within a year the east and west ends of the ground had been replaced. The final stage of major renovation work, costing £59 million, began in 1997, the funds being mostly provided by the National Lottery.

The imposing new 52,063 all-seater stadium was finally completed in time for the 1999 Scottish Cup Final. It was subsequently rated in 2002 with five stars by UEFA. Modern offices within Hampden now house the Scottish Professional Football League (SFA).

Kick-Off

'Aw, ref! Surely it's time up?' protested the Falkirk captain. 'We've already played quite a few minutes of extra time.'

'Another couple o' minutes tae go, sonny.' Erchie informed him. 'Ma watch works oan 'Fergie Time'!'

'Hey ref. You've given oot six yellow cards and a red. Yer spoilin' the game,' claimed the Rangers' captain.

'Believe me, son, ah've spoiled better games than this!' Erchie replied.

'Have ye got tae be able tae run backwards tae be a referee?' asked the cheeky faced Hibs midfielder.

'Aye, ye dae,' replied Erchie. 'And any mair nonsense oot o' you an' you'll be running backwards up that tunnel.'

The Cowdenbeath goalkeeper had let in seven goals and was clearly distraught. As Erchie gave him a sympathetic pat on the back, the goalie groaned. 'Whit a day. Imagine losing all these goals an' noo ah think ah'm going doon with the cauld.'

'At least ye were able to catch something,' consoled Erchie.

Inverness Cally were playing against Dundee United at Tannadice. The Cally manager had a quiet word in Erchie's ear prior to kick-off. 'Listen, Erchie, for heaven's sake go easy on us the day. It's tough enough playing at Tannadice, but ah've got three o' ma lads oot wi' broken bones and another four oot wi' pulled hamstrings.'

'At least yer team bus can park in a disabled space.'

'One more foul and you're on a yellow,' Erchie reprimanded the Morton striker.

'Sorry, ref. Ah'm playin' like a big Jessie today.'

'Well, in that case ye'll be the wrong sex fur any man-o'-the-match award,' quipped Erchie.

'Ref, gie's a break. Ah cannae seem tae shoot the day,' moaned the Motherwell striker.

'Yer right, son. If you'd shot at Kennedy he'd still be alive today.'

'R-e-f-e-r-e-e! You should book that midfielder. Ah think he's kicked ma bollocks aff,' moaned the Queen of the South target man, holding his groin.

'Whit dae ye want me to dae?' asked Erchie. 'Look for them?'

'Hey, referee,' growled the St Johnstone striker. 'You're not consistent with your decisions. You keep changing the goalposts.'

'Is that why ye can't get yer shots on target, sonny?'

'Ah ask ye, ref,' moaned the Dundee United striker as they both ran up the field awaiting a goal kick. 'How in the name o' the wee man did ah miss that sitter? Ah could kick masell.'

'Ah wouldnae bother. Ye'd probably miss,' smiled Erchie.

'R-e-f-e-r-e-e! You frighten the life oot o' me. Every time you're near me ah shit masell,' confided the Alloa Athletic midfield player.

'Well, just look at the money you're saving on laxative,' grinned Erchie.

'Ma manager says ah've an educated left leg,' confided the Airdrie United sweeper to Erchie as the teams trooped off at the end of the game.

'Pity the other wan didnae go tae school tae,' grinned Erchie.

The Celtic forward was known for having his brains in his feet. He had just scored a goal and was clearly exuberant about it. He whispered to Erchie. 'That's the fifteenth goal ah've scored this season, ref. That's double the number ah scored last year.'

'Just stick tae football, son,' muttered Erchie.

As the teams were leaving the field at Almondvale Stadium at the end of the match, one of the Livingston players glowered at Erchie and said, 'We wis robbed, ref. Ah'm right peeved. It wis criminal.'

'In that case if ah were you ah wid phone *Crimestoppers*.'

'Hey, r-e-f-e-r-e-e. Play fair! There are two sides playing today, ye know,' said the unhappy Stirling Albion midfielder.

'Oh, aye? Ah wis wondering when your lot would start playing.'

Temptation
Part 1

THE LOW MORNING SUN sparkled on the glass of the imposing frontage of Scotland's National Stadium, Hampden Park. It was a behemoth of power and prestige guarding the beautiful game north of the border.

The proud old lady, resplendent in her impressive finery since her 1999 refurbishment, had hosted many prestigious football finals: three Champions League Finals, two European Cup Winners' Cup finals and an UEFA cup final as well as many Scottish domestic cup finals. One of the greatest football matches ever played anywhere in the world had been held there. At the quintessential European Cup Final of 1960 a crowd of 127,000 saw Real Madrid beat Eintracht 7–3. The legendry Real maestros, Ferenc Puskas and Alfredo di Stefano, scored all seven goals for their team.

Archibald B. Smith – known to all and sundry as Big Erchie – rode into the impressive underground roadway beneath the south stand on his Harley Davidson, which he parked adjacent to a lift door. When he removed his helmet, unzipped his leather jacket and dismounted, any keen observer would have seen a small man in his early forties with a lived-in, handsome face, an obviously bullish demeanour and intense, piercing blue eyes. He was also noticeably pigeon-toed like most athletic, nimble men.

The SPFL chief executive had asked him to come in for a confidential chat. 'Ah, well,' Erchie sighed. 'Let's get it over with.' No doubt the chief wanted to indulge in a bit of hand-wringing following Erchie's sending off of six Old Firm players in the recent display of vibrant rivalry. It had unfortunately resulted in some crowd trouble. Didn't they understand that one of his greatest delights was to impose outrage and delight, in equal measure, to both sides in this chasm of intense rivalry which remained obsessive, bitter and as illogically intense as ever?

The Cup Tie had been fought out at Celtic Park on a bitterly cold day of drifting sheets of rain, with the predictive chants, baleful anthems of defiance, and gaggles of fat fans with their shirts off, waving their team colours and laughing as if to say, 'Call this cold? It's positively tropical'.

The match had ended in a draw and the replay would be the following week, hence, no doubt, the CEO's sensitivities. Indeed Erchie had to be escorted from Celtic Park by security men as a hard core of supporters from both sides seemed quite keen on lynching him. When he got to his Harley he had been met by two surly youths, their pinched faces strewn with pimples, dressed in cheap fake Nike, ubiquitous hoods and polyester trackie bottoms. Both were drawing heavily on cigarettes with the affected manner of hard men, eyes narrowed, and provoked Erchie with loud intimidating threats. Deterred by the presence of the yellow vested guards and Erchie's fearless scowl, they had backed off as he calmly mounted his motorbike and rode off along London Road.

Erchie entered the lift and hesitated briefly before pressing the button for the sixth floor where the SPFL offices were located. He knew that CCTV cameras would have filmed his entry and no doubt the security officers would have murmured, 'Here comes that wee b*****d, Big Erchie'.

Erchie smiled at the thought and pressed the lift button. But what could his masters possibly be upset about? It was absurd. All the sending offs at Celtic Park had been valid. The Referees' Supervisor was happy and even the overcritical TV pundits had agreed with his decisions. Anyway, any crowd disturbance after the sixth player had been dismissed had been a mild fracas compared to the problems of the past.

Entering the corridors of power on the sixth floor, the first person he saw was the receptionist, a petite blonde by the name of Diane. Erchie had always fancied her. Putting on a Sean Connery voice he quipped, 'Good morning, Mishh Moneypenny, James Bond at your service.'

'Mair like Premium Bond, just like yer chances!' Diane laughed. 'Erchie you really are a hoot. You always swagger in here like a western sheriff with a sort of tough, tortured look in yer eyes.'

'Aye, well let me tell you, Diane, about ma tortured look,' said Erchie with a slight grin. 'It's piles, you know, haemorrhoids. All hard men have them. Did ye ever see Gary Cooper an' Grace Kelly in *High Noon*? Cooper walked up and doon the town's street waiting for the killers, but he didnae appear feart. That wis because his face wis all screwed up in torment fae piles. His inflamed piles had him in agony. Probably while Tex Ritter was singing the theme song, and that clock on the wall was ticking, he was stuffing cream up his posterior.'

'Erchie! You're an incorrigible liar,' smiled Diane before adding, 'Do you really have piles?'

'That's a bit personal, Diane, but ah'm just at the kiddin'.'

'Erchie, you really are something else,' she giggled.

Erchie walked through the buzz and energy of the main office to the chief executive, James Barclay's suite, the echelon of power, just as the CEO himself was coming out. 'Hello, Archibald. Thanks for coming. Tell you what,' he suggested, 'why don't we go and have a coffee and chat in the cafeteria?'

Immediately Erchie knew that this was going to be a discussion and not a ticking off. Only serious problems were resolved behind closed doors. His masters' noses were not out of joint.

Over cappuccinos the chief executive of the SPFL congratulated Erchie on his firm handling of the recent Old Firm encounter. Sprawled in his seat, one arm flung over the back of the adjacent chair, short hair, looking over his glasses and distinctive dark eyebrows not quite meeting in the middle, he continued complimenting Erchie on his control of the tribal tie. In particular the sixth sending off had been much vindicated by slow-motion TV replays, some experts being amazed that Erchie's sharp eyes had spotted what had turned out to be a clear infringement of the rules. Even the Head of Referee Operations in the stand had seemed satisfied. However, as always, the SFA and SPFL were sensitive to the media and the headlines had not shown Scottish football in a good light with the same hoary old clichés.

The chief executive continued. 'What I really want to discuss with you is the forthcoming replay at Ibrox Stadium. Confidentially,' and here he dropped his voice, 'the Chief Constable has been in touch. Now, this is just between you and me, and I haven't mentioned it to our Head of Referee Operations. I know it's not the Chief Constable's business but he is suggesting that a – well – somewhat more lenient approach could be taken with offenders.' An expression of annoyance passed across Erchie's face. He and the CEO had never really rubbed along together, and he had suspected all along the flattery had been leading up to something. Now he knew why.

'It's clear to me,' continued the chief executive, 'that the Chief Constable is not a football man. Archibald, let me be honest with you, I don't want to unduly influence you. I am merely passing on the message from the police. You quite rightly interpret the rules of the game fairly and have our highest respect, but, well, you know what

Old Firm matches are like and this is a particularly mouth watering one. What do you think?'

Erchie made another grimace. He was not one for fawning or forelock-tugging to anyone. His mind seethed with frustration. 'Don't you think it would be more appropriate if the police were tae talk tae the Rangers and Celtic managers? They're the ones who tell their players to get stuck in. If ah wis overly lenient then the rest of Scottish football would surely think that something was amiss. Eh?'

'Well, you do what you think is right, Archibald. I've told you the gist of the police message. I really don't want to add anything further. So I'll leave it with you to ponder over.' Then as a sweetener he added, 'Archibald, you are a major player on the Scottish football scene. You know that. So don't be upset or take this the wrong way.'

Wrong way, thought Erchie. And I'm being encouraged to go easy on the rules. Not on your life, pal.

'Anyway,' concluded the chief. 'Would you like another coffee?'

Ah'd like a glass o' malt, thought Erchie, but he replied, 'Naw, naw, ah'm fine. Thanks.'

'Well, in that case I'll take my leave. Bye.' James Barclay rose quickly and shook Erchie's hand, leaving the referee to sit and think on the implications of their confab.

Erchie sat for a few minutes, his mind loitering over the discussion. He was perturbed. Perhaps a wander around the nearby Scottish Hall of Fame located within Hampden would settle his thoughts.

Erchie entered the Footballing Hall of Fame, looking
at the celebrated names of Scottish football's heroes.
His eye found the spot on which the famous and well
respected gentleman referee, Tom 'Tiny' Wharton's name
appeared. 'What would you do, Tiny, in my position?'
he asked. But of course he knew the answer. Tiny would
have stuck strictly to the rule book.

That very evening, Erchie was sitting in the lounge
of his flat watching recordings from *Sportscene* of
matches he had refereed, when the building security
entrance buzzer went from the external door three floors
below. He pressed the freeze button on the TV remote
and examined the security door CCTV screen. A small
man stood holding what appeared to be a case. Not
recognising the individual the referee lifted the handset
and queried, 'Can I help you?'

'I can help you, Meester Erchie,' came a silky voice he
didn't recognise. 'I weesh to discuss something important
with you.'

'Beat it, pal,' snapped Erchie, pressing the 'No Entry'
button and promptly putting down the receiver.

The buzzer went again.

Erchie decided to ignore it, but its incessant noise
forced him to once again lift the receiver.

The voice said, 'I am bringing you a present from a
friend, Meester Erchie.'

Erchie scrutinised the image on the screen. The man
appeared diminutive, darkish and thin. But he was
immediately suspicious of any 'present from a friend'...

he didn't have many. Curiosity got the better of him. On impulse he pressed the entry buzzer.

'Right, come up,' he instructed. 'You've got two minutes.'

Quickly moving into his hall cupboard, he removed a five iron from his golf bag and hid it behind the sofa in the lounge. You couldn't be too careful, nowadays.

In anticipation Erchie pulled open the front door of his flat, just as the stranger stepped out of the building's lift, carefully avoiding the various leafy plants on the hallway placed there by a neighbour.

'Good evening, Meester Erchie.' said the stranger in an accent that Erchie couldn't quite place. He was indeed small, wrinkled as a walnut and clearly of Asian stock, with dark eyes, cinnamon skin, unnaturally white teeth, and wearing a sharp, blue Armani suit.

'A lovely apartment, Meester Erchie,' he observed entering the lounge and looking keenly around. 'I would estimate an apartment like this would cost you, say, two hundred thousand of your pounds. Do you have a large mortgage on the property?'

'By heavens you're a bit forward, sunshine. That's my business,' snapped Erchie. 'What is it you want? I don't need a loan or a mortgage.'

'Well, Meester Erchie, you are the famous referee. People speak glowingly of you. Yes?'

Erchie's mouth straightened in a hard line, already regretting his decision to let this man into his flat.

'You recently refereed a football game between your Celtic and Rangers teams. Yes?'

'What about it?' growled Erchie.

'You made big news all over the world by sending off three players from each team. Yes?'

'Ur you a reporter?' queried Erchie, growing increasingly uneasy.

'No, Meester Erchie. I am, shall we say, an emissary.'

'An emissary?' queried Erchie. 'And just what organisation do you represent?'

'Dear friends from a country far away, but who love your Scottish football.'

'Are you from a supporters' club, then?'

Ignoring the question the stranger continued. 'I would make a reasonable guess that your loan on this apartment would be in the order of, perhaps fifty thousand pound. Would you agree, Meester Erchie?'

Exactly, thought Erchie, now smitten with a hollow sensation as he guessed what was coming.

'Let me be specific. Your friends, Meester Erchie,' he said with a predatory gleam in his eyes, 'will give you a nice present of fifty thousand pounds, in cash. All you have to do is, in the coming match, again send off three players from each side. Easy money, Meester Erchie.'

Erchie was slack-jawed in disbelief at this bombshell. He had heard of referees in Europe being offered bribes to fix matches but here he was, Archibald B. Smith, now experiencing this at first hand.

'Get out, ya wee swine!' shouted Erchie. 'How dare you come in here and offer me dirty money to make your gambling friends a fortune. Out! Now!'

'I will go,' said the smiling, furtive stranger. 'But just let me show you what fifty thousand pounds looks like,' and he unzipped his bag.

Erchie had a quick glance at a shedload of fifty pound notes.

'Out!' shouted a red faced Erchie, moving towards the sofa where the five iron lay.

'I contact you soon, Meester Erchie,' smiled the stranger backing out of the door. 'Maybe you should think carefully about this very kind offer.'

Erchie slammed his front door and stood for a moment trying to calm down. He dimly heard the lift descending. On impulse he grabbed his cagoule and house keys. Scurrying down the building's stairs he arrived on the pavement outside just in time to see the stranger entering the front passenger door of a Mercedes saloon. It took off at some speed, but not before Erchie had noted its registration.

He returned to his apartment, somewhat shaken. The television was switched off and he poured himself a generous malt.

Fifty thousand to become as crooked as the people this guy represents. How dare they, thought Erchie, his mind in turmoil. He looked at the many photographs adorning his wall, highlights and controversial moments in games plus images capturing him received medals for refereeing finals. A feeling of lassitude suddenly overwhelmed him.

It was an hour later before the television was turned

back on, but his thoughts were mostly elsewhere. Heavens above, he thought. On one hand he had the CEO telling him the police suggested going easy on bookings, and on the other hand he was being offered money to send off another six players. This couldn't be happening to him, surely?

His scalp prickled with unease.

The following day was a busy one at the practice where he worked as an accountant. Although Erchie was kept occupied with various clients his thoughts drifted back to the previous evening's encounter. It was an exhausting day and darkness had fallen together with steady rain by the time he returned home.

As he approached the entry to his block of flats Erchie got a surprise. From the shadows emerged the stranger from the previous night, but this time a woman was standing behind him. Deceived by the damp, jostling shadows of passing cars, all he could see of her was long, blonde hair.

'Meester, Erchie,' began the stranger, but he got no further before Erchie interjected.

'Ah told you tae piss aff last night, sunshine!' bellowed Erchie.

'This conversation would really be better in the privacy of your accommodation, Meester Erchie. But give me just one minute. I represent powerful but generous people. Our offer to you is now increased. In addition to the money, Suzie here will spend a night with you to demonstrate her, shall we say, not inconsiderable charms. You are a good looking man, Meester Erchie. You like women. Yes? This is a sort of, shall we say, package offer.' He smiled conspiratorially.

Erchie was taken aback, but had to admit to himself that any red-blooded man would be tempted.

'Get out of my sight both of you before I call the police,' he shouted.

'We will go now, Meester Erchie. Oh, by the way. Look, Meester Erchie, what is that across your road?'

Erchie automatically turned and as he did so was startled by the flash from a camera.

Erchie was stunned. 'Ya sleekit wee b*****d!' he bellowed.

Quickly the couple turned and moved off down the road, the stranger stopping for a moment to turn around and shout. 'I will phone you, Meester Erchie.'

They disappeared from sight around a corner, and a glance to the other side of the road showed Erchie that their accomplice had also gone.

Erchie stood, dumfounded at the audacity of it all.

In a daze he entered his flat and poured himself a malt with shaky hands, before sitting down heavily on a chair. It was half-an-hour and two further malts before he even thought of food.

The last thing he wanted was any involvement with a gambling syndicate. A fifty thousand bribe, no way. A night with this Suzie... well. But he quickly dismissed this foolish thought. But now this organisation had a photograph of him no doubt apparently appearing in cahoots with the pair. They were clearly trying to implicate him. These audacious people must represent a seriously major gambling operation.

A cloud of apprehension hung over him. Perhaps this was all his own doing. The high profile he loved and indeed had nourished with the Scottish media had brought him to their attention. The whole thing gave him the heebie-jeebies and he let out a huge shuddering sigh.

Gradually his mood of apprehension gave way to one of seething resentment at being placed in this position.

Hunger finally got to him. Five minutes later he found himself luxuriating in the smell of his local chippy with its glass counter and fried fish, sausages and burgers all in neat glistening rows under the red-hot strip of the steel counter. It was when he was later cramming his mouth with chips and piping hot battered cod that he finally made his decision. Really he should have done this when approached the previous night. His greasy face lit up. How dare they have the temerity to try and co-opt him into their scheme. He would hand the whole thing over to his bosses at Hampden. Let them deal with it.

The following morning before setting off for the office Erchie, as usual, checked his mail box. A quick flick revealed junk mail with only two envelopes of any consequence. One a reminder to go for his yearly eye test at Specsavers. He decided to leave it for a while. There was also a large brown envelope containing a photograph of Erchie and the couple standing together. Although the image wasn't sharp, there appeared to be a large smile on the emissary's face. Erchie slumped against the mail box, hands trembling. 'Swine,' he muttered.

From work, an extremely angry Erchie phoned through to Hampden and spoke directly to James Barclay. He reminded Barclay of the conversation they had recently and then went on to explain how an approach had been made to him to do exactly the opposite. He suggested an urgent meeting, recommending that police representatives be present. The CEO readily agreed and the meeting was quickly set up for later that very morning.

A few hours later Erchie made his way out to Hampden on his Harley Electra Glide using a circuitous route, continually looking in his mirrors as he weaved speedily through traffic, cutting past cars to the front at red lights, and bringing up the rpm to take sudden turns onto minor roads, all to ensure he wasn't being followed.

In a small conference room Erchie was introduced by James Barclay to two burly, broad-shouldered police-men. Chief Superintendent MacAuley , a florid faced dour individual and DI Jamieson, a rubicund, craggy, middle-aged chap who smiled and whose firm handshake gave Erchie some reassurance although the band of a signet ring pressed heavily into Erchie's little finger. Good cop, bad cop, thought Erchie. The referee spent some time going over every detail of his encounter, showing them the photograph and answering their questions as he went along. Jamieson made notes, occasionally tapping a pen against his teeth. James Barclay sat listening, his fingers pressed together, immersed in thought.

'Mmm,' commented an unsmiling Chief Super MacAuley, now sprawled in his seat. 'This is extremely serious. The chap is clearly an intermediary. To be frank with you the jungle drums have been warning us for some time that this kind of malarkey was afoot and an approach might be made to people in Scottish football. They certainly made a mistake in approaching you, Erchie, with your reputation as a hard man who stands no nonsense.'

'They appear to be a determined lot, obviously keen to relieve bookies of more money than is decent withoot a gun,' said Erchie with a bitter grin.

'Well, there is one thing for sure,' observed James Barclay in a gravelly undertone. 'Erchie cannot possibly referee this replay.' Then turning to Erchie he said,' Don't worry, we'll say you are ill or something, Archibald. We certainly don't want anyone thinking you were dropped.'

'That's for you to decide, James,' said Jamieson, 'but it does seem the sensible thing. I would certainly love to catch this bunch of dodgy characters. They mustn't be allowed to featherbed themselves on our patch. By the way, while you were talking I texted in the vehicle registration you gave. It's from a stolen car, so no luck there, I'm afraid.'

'Well, they're goin' tae contact me again tae see if

ah've changed ma mind.' said Erchie. 'So ah need you guys tae guide me on what ah should do next.'

'Tell you what,' suggested the Chief Super, 'when they do, why don't you say that you have thought it all over. What they are asking is for you to put your whole career at risk. You might even go to jail. So you want a hundred thousand, with half up front. After all, if you had been doing what they ask, it seems likely you would never have heard from them again.'

'And what if they agree, Superintendent?' queried Erchie.

'Oh, they'll probably agree, Erchie,' continued the policeman. 'Perhaps not to an extra fifty thousand but no doubt to a lesser sum to seal the deal, though I think you should hold out for fifty. And don't worry, in no way will this be considered condoning criminality.'

'Listen, Erchie,' interjected DI Jamieson. 'What we'll do is supply you with another mobile in case they are hacking into yours. Assuming the deal is on, then you can let us know when and where you'll get the cash. Our boys will be waiting to swoop. The only problem is you may be putting yourself in harm's way. Are you quite happy to go through with this?'

'Listen,' replied a grinning Erchie, 'compared to an Old Firm match it will be a doddle.'

Jamieson raised his eyebrows in admiration. 'Aye, well, good point, Erchie. I guess no right thinking person would have the temerity to take issue with you. So, fine. We're all agreed on our plan of action, that is, assuming your CEO here is happy to let his top referee carry this out.'

'Reluctantly, I am,' replied James Barclay. 'We certainly don't want this sort of thing to infiltrate the Scottish game.'

That night Erchie was on tenterhooks. The television was off, and he hadn't put on his favourite Elgar CDs. He sat silently, glancing intermittently at his own mobile on the coffee table beside which sat the newly supplied mobile from the police.

His reverie was interrupted by his own mobile ringing. 'We are carrying out a survey in your area on double-glazing…' Erchie immediately cut off the voice. 'Thanks a lot for nothing, pal,' he muttered angrily.

No sooner had he put the instrument down when it rang again. Erchie took a deep breath and pressed the 'on' button. 'Yes,' he growled.

Once again he heard the silky tone. 'Ah, Meester Erchie,' the voice began. 'we hope you are in good spirits and ready to make us all very happy and rich.'

'Maybe,' said Erchie slowly.

'That sounds promising, Meester Erchie.'

'Right. I've thought about your, erm, tantalising offer very carefully, but ah'm worried. You must appreciate ah would be takin' a major risk that could mean ah end up in prison. So, ah want a hundred thousand pounds and an advance of money before ah do what you want.'

'No problem, Meester Erchie. We will give you, say, twenty thousand pounds up front.'

'Not nearly enough, my friend,' Erchie said. 'Ah want half.'

'That is a lot of money, Meester Erchie.'

'It is. But ah'm perfectly aware that once the game is over ah may never hear from you again.'

'I represent very honest people, Meester Erchie.'

Aye, that'll be right, thought Erchie.

'Hold on Meester Erchie.'

Erchie could hear distant voices conversing in a language he couldn't identify.

'Very well, Meester Erchie. We agree to your demand. I will bring you the money tomorrow night to your apartment.'

'Mmmm. Can we not meet somewhere else?'

'Like where, Meester Erchie?'

'How about the food court in Princes Square, just off Buchanan Street in Glasgow city centre?'

'Why there, Meester Eechie?'

'Well, it's where ah have lunch most days. And it's popular and busy with shoppers having snacks. You'll see me sitting at a table and then you can just pass me the money. Easy.'

There was some hesitation before the reply came. 'All right, Meester Erchie. Tomorrow then, at what time?'

'One o'clock. Thirteen hundred hours.'

'I will see you there, Meester Erchie.' And the phone clicked off.

Erchie immediately phoned DI Jamieson with the details of the drop.

The following lunchtime found Erchie sitting at a table in the food court on the top level of Princes Square, slowly munching his favourite 'Glasgow salad' – an artery-furring plate of chips. Ah certainly didn't expect to be caught up in nonsense like this when ah became a referee, he thought.

Anxiously glancing around, he was unable to spot anyone who remotely looked like a police officer. Nothing but the usual frenzy of jostling shoppers, young wives with prams, and the continual hum of conversation.

Finishing his 'salad', he slowly sipped his tea and tried to read the sports section of *The Herald*, but his thoughts were elsewhere and he didn't take in the words. A quick glance at his watch showed it was now ten past one.

He's late for this rendezvous, thought Erchie.

When it came to half-past one he came to the conclusion the deal was off for some reason or other, leaving him somewhat bemused and with the beginning of a nagging ache at the top of his skull. Anyway, he now had to get back to the office. Rising he gifted his table to a grateful diner and made his way out while wondering if he had got the timing wrong. It had certainly not gone according to plan, thought Erchie, turning the ever-multiplying complexities of the situation over in his mind.

As he navigated homewards that evening bestride his Harley along the asphalt of Great Western Road, zig-zagging in and out of a continuous stream of slow noisy traffic, his mind was continually going over the situation. It was at this point he heard his Bluetooth go off. Clicking it on, he heard the familiar glib voice through the speaker in the carbon fibres of his helmet.

'Meester Erchie?'

'Aye, it's me. Ye didnae turn up, sunshine.'

'Oh, but I did, Meester Erchie. I was there from noon until two o'clock.'

'So how come you didn't give me the money, eh?'

'Oh, but I had to ensure you were, shall we say, unaccompanied. Your change of venue could have been a ploy. We are very careful people, you know.'

'Of course ah was on my own!' protested Erchie indignantly.

'You were, Meester Erchie. So I can only apologise for the slight hitch in our arrangement, but one cannot be too careful, nowadays. There are a lot of criminals around,' he laughed.

'Well, sunshine, it's simple. No money no deal,' said Erchie, carefully weaving his way through a traffic-snarled Anniesland Cross.

'Tomorrow, Meester Erchie. Same place, but at three o'clock.' And before Erchie could reply the line went dead.

At home he spent some time on the police mobile filling DI Jamieson in with the new arrangements. Then he phoned and updated CEO James Barclay.

The following afternoon at three o'clock, Erchie once more found himself in the relaxed, yet vibrant Princes Square food court. Looking around he was worried. It was the middle of the afternoon and there were fewer people eating, unlike the usual lunchtime activity. And where were the police? Nothing but young wives with children and prams, together with some older couples obviously taking a rest from their shopping.

Just then he felt a tap on his shoulder and was conscious that a bag had been slipped under his chair. Glancing up he saw a young man of Asian appearance. Erchie opened his mouth to speak but the fellow was not for stopping and took off. The 'errand boy' had scarpered no more than a dozen quick steps before a pram suddenly blocked his path while another slipped in behind him. Erchie sat impressed as two young, smartly dressed 'mums' tripped the delivery boy, put him in a headlock and snapped on handcuffs. Two 'male assistants' materialised from behind the counter of an adjacent restaurant and marched the fellow off.

Feeling a sudden moment of triumph Erchie picked up the bag, but before he had any opportunity to examine its contents a hand was placed on his shoulder. 'Sorry, Erchie,' laughed DI Jamieson. 'but you cannae keep it.'

'Pity,' replied Erchie looking up at the smiling face. 'I was sort of hoping it could go tae a good cause.'

Jamieson grinned again with bemused benevolence, 'Don't worry, Erchie, it will. All proceeds from crime now go back into the community.'

The commotion had quickly died down. All of the police officers disappeared, and the referee was left conscious of passers by eyeing him suspiciously while pointing him out to their friends. Erchie quickly slipped out before someone thought of phoning the newspapers.

Temptation
Part 2

THE CUP TIE between Celtic and Rangers took place on a Wednesday night with an eight o'clock kick off. A large contingent of police and security men were on duty and, as expected, the match was a sell-out. Tribesmen from both sides had gathered to worship their creeds with rousing songs of battle, hatred and blood. A palpable loathing of mass aggression manifested itself over each end of a stadium containing no neutral fans.

Erchie sat with a large glass of Glenmorangie in his hand in front of the television and watched the gladiatorial contest between the battle-hardened adversaries.

He wondered how his replacement, Sammy McGill, would handle the game. After half-an hour of play it was obvious that Sammy was standing no nonsense. Each side had contributed to the gore and carnage and both had a player sent off. There were also a number of players on yellow cards. By half-time Rangers had another man sent off and were down to nine men. The score was one all.

It was clear in the second half that the players had been lectured on their discipline at half-time. Only a few more shin-kicking contests still prevailed. Despite virtually all-out attack by Celtic, Rangers scored on a breakaway. This was to prove decisive as the Ibrox men gave a desperate backs-to-the-wall performance. Erchie listened to the usual post mortem by former players of both clubs, before switching off.

The following day was an extremely busy one at work. In addition he had to take a couple of hours off to make a final statement to the police. DI Jamieson had been extremely pleased. He told a reassured Erchie that the 'delivery boy' had 'sung' in the hope of a lighter sentence, and as a result they had managed to catch the gang, with the exception of the woman.

That night, following a few unwinding malts, Erchie opted to have an early night. He had to admit to himself that the whole experience had been quite stressful. It was at this point that the building entry buzzer signalled the arrival of a visitor. Looking into the small screen he saw it was the woman 'on offer' from the gang. She said, 'I come to make you happy man, Meester Erchie'.

There was no one else showing up on the security screen and he was suddenly overly conscious of the luscious blonde hair. On impulse, and aided by the drink, he pressed the entry button.

Am ah gonnae regret this? he wondered, while another part of him thought on the potential delights on offer.

He heard the lift stop outside his flat and opened the front door. 'Did they no' tell you the deal wis off?' he immediately queried.

'Off? Off? They no tell me. Anyways, I like you, Meester Erchie.'

Erchie became aware that the voice he had initially thought might be alluring and sultry had clearly been acquired by a lifetime of cigarettes. The stretched vowels and excruciating accent suddenly annoyed him.

As she moved nearer the light from his hallway he realised with a shock that this was no sparkling, beguiling creature, certainly no young dolly bird. It had only been the blonde hair that had made her seem attractive.

Erchie hesitated for only a moment before saying, 'No thanks, dear. Sorry, a wee misunderstanding,' and quietly closed the door.

'Should've Gone tae Specsavers,' he muttered.

Yellow Cards

The Hibs player was injured. He had badly hurt his ankle and was distraught as he was carried off during the match at Paisley. 'It's no' fair,' he moaned to Erchie. 'Ye gave me a yellow card, then ah get hurt, and wid you believe this is ma Saint's day.'

'You never know, you might get a ride tae the hospital in a St John's ambulance driven by a St Mirren supporter!'

'Ref! You're as thick as mince!' shouted the angry Albion Rovers forward who had just seen his goal disallowed.

'Right, three things, sunshine,' said Erchie testily. 'Firstly, whit's yer name? Secondly, you're now on a yellow. And thirdly, ye should change yer butcher!'

'Ref, that wisnae a penalty,' protested the Stranraer defender. 'The only dirty thing ah've done aw day wis fart.'

'Well it wis certainly a stinkin' tackle,' smiled Erchie grimly. 'Yellow card!'

'Right, whit's yer name, Cinderella?' asked Erchie.

'Ma name isnae Cinderella,' protested the Peterhead defender.

'Well, aw ye seem tae dae efter kickin' everybody is run away fae the ball. And you cannae have a very good coach!'

'That was never a penalty, referee,'
moaned the Partick Thistle central midfielder.
'Away an' take a running jump intae the Clyde.'

'Aye, well you actually remind me o' the Clyde,
sunshine. Small at the heid and big at the mooth.
Yellow card!' said Erchie.

'But referee', protested Arbroath's target man.
'Maradona got away wi' it. He said it wis the
hand o' God.'

'Well, yours wis the hand o' a right bampot.
Yellow card!' grinned Erchie.

'Aw, ref. Ah jist stuck oot ma foot an' the ba' hit me oan the arm,' protested the St Johnstone defender.

'Well, ye'll jist need tae take this yellow card oan the chin, sonny.'

'Aw, r-e-f-e-r-e-e. Gie's a break. Ah'm only seventeen,' claimed the young Clyde right back.

'Whit dae ye want me tae dae... change yer nappy, sonny? This is a man's game. Yellow card!'

'Any mair nonsense, Humpty Dumpty and you're on a red card,' Ernie told the Queen's Park defender as he held up a yellow card.

'Ma name's no' Humpty Dumpty, referee.'

'Well, if ye keep on foulin' you're in for a great fall, Humpty.'

'Right, sunshine, whit's yer name?' Erchie asked the Montrose forward.

'Chancellor.'

'Chancellor?'

'Aye, like the guy in charge of the government's money.'

'Well, you've overtaxed ma patience today, Mister Chancellor. Yellow card!'

The game between Aberdeen and Inverness Cally was fast and furious.

Just before half-time Erchie awarded a penalty to Inverness Cally. The Aberdeen captain ran after Erchie and complained. 'Listen, ref, I can't believe you gave that as a penalty.'

'Well, sunshine, if you read the Sunday papers tomorrow you'll find out ah did!'

The St Mirren midfielder had made a few sarcastic comments to Erchie during much of the first-half. Then, during a sudden attack, an opposing St Johnstone forward was left sprawling on the grass by the midfield player. Erchie welcomed the opportunity.

'Right, whit's yer name, Mister Comedian?'

'Me? Ah'm Joseph King,' said the player with a smug smile.

'Well you might be Joe King but ah'm no' joking. Yellow card, and if you don't keep yer big mouth closed it wull be a red next time.'

Big Erchie and Gazza

IF ERCHIE HAD DECIDED TO GO straight home after his training session, or if he had opted for a coffee in Costa, or if he had even thought of a few holes of golf, it would have been okay. But fate was not quite on his side that particular day, when he walked, unwittingly, into the moribund lounge of The Victorian and Albert Vaults for a beer. He should have known by its shabby, litter-strewn doorway that it would be a comfortless den dedicated to pool, TV sport and the consumption of strong lager, fortified wine and deep fried crisps.

Custom was slack, and the atmosphere chill. As he stood at the bar quietly sipping his brew, a huge man staggered over to Erchie with the exaggerated ceremony of the inebriated and a cock o' the walk assurance, and put a massive paw on his shoulder. Erchie looked up into a mouth containing three teeth, a blackened one in the middle and two decidedly yellow gnashers on either side, set in a florid face of broken-veined puffiness and with all the menace of a psychotic gorilla.

'Ur you that wee b*****d, Big Erchie, the so-called referee?'

Erchie cast an eye around the bar already regretting his decision to nip into this particular pub in a soulless part of the city for a quick pint. The barman, an individual with a moustache which reminded the referee of a certain Austrian housepainter, had suddenly stopped polishing glasses and was peering at a mobile which he now had in his hand. Erchie wondered if he was phoning for an ambulance. Other drinkers had suddenly moved away to form an impromptu gathering at the far end of the bar where they huddled in anticipation of some pending action.

'Dae ye no' hear me, ya wee twat?' came the intimidating voice. It was accompanied by a menacing whiff of halitosis and alcohol from an unsmiling expression suggesting barely concealed aggression. The fellow hawked up some phlegm and spat on the floor.

Erchie smiled tolerantly, cast him a wary look and suddenly asked. 'Dae you remember Gazza, big man?'

'Whit! Gazza? Of course ah dae. Played fur Rangers. Whit aboot him?' slurred the drunk.

'Well, this will bring back memories,' said Erchie, his strong right hand at the same time grabbing the brute's testicles. Strength, much helped by many early years on a farm, held a firm grip on the vital, vulnerable parts.

'Dae ye no' remember Vinnie Jones once had Gazza by the balls? There wis a famous photo taken at the time o' the incident,' explained Erchie, while looking up intently at his victim.

The now white face nodded, the fleshy jowls slackened and the mouth fell part open in pain and disbelief.

'Aye, the incident got a lot of publicity,' remarked Erchie, and then with his left hand slowly drained the remainder of his glass.

'Nice to have met you,' smiled Erchie, his still, steady

gaze never faltering. 'It's good to talk about the old days in football, sure it is?'

Another strained nod.

'Cheerio, then,' said Erchie, giving the fellow's testicles a final, massive squeeze.

Erchie, wearing a mirthless smile, calmly nodded to the barman and steered an evasive course past the pool table to the door, leaving the giant doubled in two and the clientele agog.

* * *

'Do you want the good news or the bad news, Erchie?' the voice on the other end of the phone asked.

'Give us the bad news.'

'Well, Erchie,' came the executive from the SPFL. 'We've had the *Daily Record* and the *Edinburgh Evening News* on about this pub assault.'

'Whit pub assault?' asked Erchie, immediately guessing what it was about.

'Erchie, you were in a pub in Glasgow and allegedly attacked another drinker. The barman phoned the media looking for a couple of hundred quid for the story. The papers are wanting a comment.'

'How about blatantly untrue, puerile and slanderous?' said Erchie, quickly realising that shock and confusion are no friends to clear thinking.

'Sounds a reasonable line, Erchie, but what actually happened?'

'Ah was having a quiet pint in a pub while talking to a football fan about famous players, like Gazza. The fellow looked a bit, shall we say, sick, so ah left. Obviously somebody has misinterpreted the situation.'

'Apparently there are witnesses, Erchie.'

'So why has no one called the polis, then?'

'I believe the police have been informed, Erchie.'

Erchie sighed heavily. 'Aw, naw. Looks like I'll never have ma name up on that Scottish Hall of Fame wall at Hampden.'

'Well, it depends how this pans out, Erchie. You'll need to talk yourself out of this one. You might be suspended in the meantime if there is to be a court case, I don't know. Please keep me up to date if there are any developments. And by the way, there's no good news.'

The line clicked off at the other end before a perplexed Erchie could utter his reply of 'surely someone is innocent until proved otherwise.' He was worried by the situation and troubled by the inflection in the executive's voice.

The following day was Monday. It was nearing the end of the tax year and the accountancy office was busy. Midway through the morning, a secretary popped her head round his office door to announce that a couple of policemen were in the foyer, and they wanted a word.

Erchie sighed, and wearily made his way out to the reception desk in the foyer, fretful of the two flint-faced policemen who awaited him.

'Good morning, gentlemen,' said Erchie somewhat

apprehensively. The duo rose and duly accompanied him into a warren of small conference rooms used for interviewing clients. They entered the first one which was free.

Both policemen sat stony faced, hats on laps, notebooks and pens at the ready.

One looked rather small to be a constable, was barrel-chested, had a shaven head, darting eyes and appeared to be nearing retirement. The other was clearly taller, younger, and running to fat with dark greasy hair and a plaster on the side of his cheek, no doubt, thought Erchie, as the result of dealing with a recent fracas.

They looked bored and, if anything, hostile.

'We are investigating the circumstances of a complaint made by a customer in a Glasgow public house. He alleges he was the victim of an assault by yourself. Could you shed any light on this, sur?'

'Well, I'm gobsmacked', began Erchie. 'This is ridiculous. As you gents might well appreciate when ye are a well kent referee then it's an occupational hazard going intae a pub. The last thing ye want to do is antagonise drunks. Ah know the guy yer probably talkin' aboot an' he wis as funny as leprosy, an' certainly didnae like ma humour. Came over tae talk to me when ah wis havin' a pint on ma oan.'

'I appreciate that you have a reputation for humour, sur, but this is a serious investigation,' stated the policeman, a pursing of his lips hinting at some irritation. 'So can you tell me what happened in this incident, sur?'

'Well, ah widnae call it an incident,' smiled Erchie

tolerantly. 'We, err, not surprisingly got onto the subject of football and talked aboot Gazza, you know, Paul Gascoigne who played for a number of teams, including Rangers.'

'The gentleman making the accusation alleges you deliberately assaulted him, sur.'

'The guy was obviously very drunk, officers, and I doubt his recollection of our wee chat would be very clear. The human mind can be complex and perverse.'

'Well, sur, he has said in his statement, which I have here,' and he looked down at his notebook. 'that you deliberately held and squeezed his testicles.'

'Ah, what the poor chap is talking about is the time Gazza was held by the balls by Vinnie Jones. At that time Gazza was playing for Newcastle and Jones for Wimbledon. Sure, ah demonstrated this to him.'

'Did he threaten you, sur?' the policeman asked with a glowering expression.

'Ah don't mind chin-waggin' about the old days in football with anybody. You know, a bit of nostalgia, but this guy's language was a wee bit intimidating. Called me a b*****d and a twat. Usually it's players or managers who call me that. I would also state that it was clear from the demeanour of the other patrons in the hostelry that they were expecting some sort of altercation. Probably this fellow has a reputation for intimidation and violence.'

'So, do you admit that you assaulted this man, sur.'

'Most certainly not,' replied Erchie, hoping his

stubborn insistence and protestations of innocence would impress on the sullen policemen that there was no case whatsoever to answer. 'It was merely a demonstration of the Gazza and Jones bit of fun. But, as ah saw the guy's attitude was threatening, ah drank up and got out. It's amazing how there can be differing perceptions of the same situation.'

The officers glanced at each other. There was a definite air of cool about their chillingly humourless expressions. Anxiety filled Erchie. They had remained impassive and weren't going to be fobbed off by his faltering explanation. They simply didn't believe him.

Erchie cleared his throat and spoke through clenched teeth. 'Let me make it clear, gents. This guy is a pathetic cretin. There is not a kernel of truth in his assertions. Ah now find myself struggling with the twin compulsions of outrage and reasonableness.'

'Thank you for your time, sur. You will no doubt be hearing further about the situation,' communicated the younger policeman as they both took a stilted farewell, leaving behind a dispirited Erchie.

* * *

Erchie's lawyer, Alistair Dodds, a spectacularly plump, pinch-faced individual of indeterminate age with piercing eyes, was a partner in the firm of Dodds and Graham Solicitors. What Erchie liked about him was that he was usually perceptive without being presumptuous, with a lively mind and penetrating intelligence. Sitting on a large buttoned-leather chair in his spacious sanctum of neatly ordered papers and plush-carpeted quietude, he observed, 'You see Erchie, what I've discovered over the time I've dealt with the police is that they don't always see past the ends of their noses unless they are fast-track management material, and that certainly doesn't sound like the pair who interviewed you in this case. He laughed. 'No doubt they're football fans keen to concoct a case against you.

'The problem is that the law here in Scotland is sometimes stubbornly impervious to certain situations. Take yours. It's obvious to a blind man running for a bus that this thug was on the point of assaulting you. Then you took what you believed to be, shall we say, appropriate action. However, sometimes common sense is not part of our law process,' he smiled ruefully. 'Furthermore, it can take the Prosecutor's office some time before they make up their mind on cases. Indecision's a real bugbear in the courts at present.'

'Can't we prepare a counterattack?' asked Erchie.

'Great idea, Erchie. A real humdinger if I may say so. But you're right, so let's prepare for the worst. Are any of the customers in this establishment likely to support an argument of self-defence?'

'I doubt it,' replied Erchie. 'They're probably all football punters, so I'll not exactly be Mister Popular, and anyway they no doubt enjoy a bit of malarkey in their local. Besides, the accuser is a menacing big sod and I'm sure retribution would be dished out to anyone supporting my defence.'

'Unfortunately, I have to agree with you,' said Alistair. 'Rather than plead self-defence I think we have got to pin our hopes on the situation you stated. Simply that you were talking of footballing bygone days and you were merely demonstrating the Gazza incident to this football fan. Mind you, Erchie, I must say that frankly I would take that with a massive pinch of salt. But hopefully the Sheriff will give your story more credence than I do. If he gives you a 'Go directly to jail do not pass go' card then you're in trouble as I don't have any magic 'Get out of jail free' cards, Erchie.'

Erchie winced and let out a gasp. 'Surely jail isn't a possibility?'

'Unlikely, but you never know when well-known personalities are in the dock and your argument is somewhat on the weak side. You may have to adjust your expectations, Erchie. However there is no use in worrying right now. First of all we need to know how the land lies. At least the SPFL have not suspended you from refereeing in the meantime. They're obviously waiting to see what happens in court.' he said.

'If I hear any more about the situation I will contact you, and if you get a summons to appear in court please inform me immediately. And another thing, don't talk to the press.'

* * *

It was just over three weeks later that the outside buzzer went in Erchie's apartment and a voice announced he was a court officer with a summons for Mister Smith.

Archie's heart sank. This could be the end of both his career as a referee and his day job as an accountant.

Upon studying the summons Erchie found out that he had to appear the following week in court to face a charge of common assault. He contacted Alistair Dodds and gave him the specific details.

'I'm assuming that you haven't changed you position on this, Erchie, and want to plead not guilty.'

'I certainly do.'

'Right, I'll put forward that plea on your behalf, and let you know when the case in front of the Sheriff will take place.'

'Can we get this thing over as quickly as possible, Alistair? The papers are full of it. Even the fans have started chanting, "Big Erchie's goin tae the jail!"'

'Okay. So what witnesses do you want to appear on your behalf?'

'I don't have anybody. You'll just have to do your best for me, Alistair,' replied Erchie lugubriously.

'See you in court, Erchie. We'll need to keep all our fingers crossed.'

* * *

It was a drizzly, clammy Tuesday morning, the greyness of the day somewhat intensified by the atmosphere prevailing in the courtroom. The public gallery was filled with a humdrum assortment of public and press, all eager to hear the case details. On the bench was Sheriff Donaldson, tight lipped and frowning, the folds of flesh on his face suggesting that this was a far from common expression. His eyes, gleaming behind heavy framed glasses, were apparently fixed on the accused in the dock.

The first witness called by the prosecution lawyer was the alleged victim, a certain Tam McDonahue. His story was that he had been chatting to the accused about football when something he had said must have upset Big Erchie, for the referee grabbed him by the balls. 'Ah know he has a reputation as a wee hard man but ah didnae think he wid attack me like that,' protested McDonahue.

'Did you at any time threaten the accused, Mister McDonahue?'

'Naw, naw. Ah'm a peace lovin' man.' This caused some irascible laughter from the public area.

It was now Alistair Dodds turn.

'Are you aware of the famous football photograph of Paul Gascoigne whose sobriquet of Gazza is well known, and another footballer, Vinnie Jones, in which Jones is apparently making Gascoigne's eyes water with a strategically placed grip?'

'Aye, ah've seen that photo in the papers.'

'Then surely you can accept that Mister Smith was merely acting out this event?'

'Naw, it wis sore.'

'But you are a man of considerable size, Mister McDonahue, whereas Mister Smith is only five feet five inches.'

'Ah don't care whit size he is, he's a wee effin' b*****d!'

At this Sheriff Donaldson intervened. 'This is a court of law, Mister McDonahue. Any more of that contemptuous language in my court and I will put you in a holding cell for a few hours to calm you down.'

'Ach, that wid be easy-peesy, pal. Ah've done two long stretches in Barlinnie afore noo!' shouted the accuser.

Sheriff Donaldson appeared to have difficulty controlling himself. 'I will not have this behaviour in court. Take him down to the cells. I hope this will be a salutary lesson to you.' Two policemen duly escorted a struggling McDonahue from the courtroom.

'Do you have any further witnesses?' the Sheriff enquired of the prosecuting counsel.

'Just the barman of the pub where the alleged assault took place, Sheriff.'

'Right, let's hear what the fellow has to say.'

The barman was duly called. As he was going up the stairs to the witness box he tripped, only saving himself from a nasty fall at the last minute. In the box he looked around, apparently very unsure of his surroundings.

'Mister Evans,' the prosecuting lawyer began, 'first of all could you point out the gentlemen who allegedly carried out the assault in your pub.'

Evans looked around, eyes peering at various people in the courtroom.

'Him,' he said, pointing to a court clerk quietly sitting writing.

At this the Sheriff intervened. 'Mister Evans, in order to clarify the situation would you once more identify the gentleman whom you allege assaulted Mister McDonahue.'

'It's him. That wee fella there,' the barman repeated, again pointing to the sitting clerk.

By now the Sheriff had gone red in the face. 'This is another example of a trivial case being brought to my court which should never have reached this stage,' he raged. 'It is obvious that the accuser is nothing more than an attention-seeking, foulmouthed nuisance. I am dismissing this case against Mister Smith forthwith on the grounds of insufficient evidence.' Erchie gave a grateful nod of acceptance.

As Erchie was leaving the courthouse, Sheriff Donaldson tapped him on the shoulder. 'If it hadn't been for those two idiots today, it would have been me giving you a yellow card,' the Sheriff winked, and then added, 'Keep up the good work.'

'Aye,' muttered Erchie, 'that numpty of a barman should've gone tae Specsavers.'

Red Cards

'But ye cannae send me aff, referee,'
moaned the East Stirlingshire striker.
'Ah've scored two goals an' ah feel ah'm oan
a hat trick.'

'Believe me, son,' retorted Erchie.
'The only way you could make a hat trick
today is if ye were a magician. Aff!'

'You're a bit o' a clown today, ref, wi' aw yer
decisions,' snarled the attention-seeking,
foul-mouthed Berwick Rangers winger.

'Ah'm no' a clown, sonny. You are. Ye see,
ah'm the ringmaster. Aff!' Erchie smiled grimly,
holding up a red card.

Erchie produced a flash of red. 'But ah'm jist a trialist, referee,' pleaded the Brechin City defender.

'In that case, son, you should plead guilty tae that two footed foul. Aff!'

'Ref, please don't send me aff,' implored the Stenhousemuir midfielder. 'Ah absolutely eat, drink and sleep football.'

'Well, it's a great pity ye cannae play it. Aff!'

'Don't ye think yer a bit card-happy today, referee? Ur ye trying to get intae the *Guinness Book of Records* for having dished out mair red cards than onybody else?' snarled the Montrose attacking midfielder.

'Good idea, sonny,' repled Erchie. 'An' you've jist helped me reach ma target. Aff!'

'Ah reckon you're nothing but a homer, referee!' moaned the Hearts player at Celtic Park.

'Aye, an' that's where you're goin' early. Aff!

'Ref, yer useless! The only thing you've got right the day wis the minute silence,' observed the Dundee sweeper.

'Aye, ah'm really good at telling the time. It's time someone told you that you would dae well tae keep quiet fur a minute. Aff... red card!'

Erchie called the Forfar player over. 'Ah can see you're no' the brightest, son, so give me a number between one and three.'

'Two, ref.'

'Exactly right. You've now got two yellow cards. Aff!'

'But, referee,' protested the slightly built Queen of the South forward. 'Give me a break. Ah'm only sixteen an' ma mother's here at the game today.'

'Sorry, sonny. It wis a dangerous two-footed tackle with your studs showing. Anyway, it's past yer bedtime an' yer mother can take ye hame an' tuck ye in. Aff!'

'How much are the Huns payin' ye, ref?' asked the Celtic midfielder.

'Not as much as that comment jist cost you.' snapped Erchie. 'Aff!'

It was the Scottish Cup Final at Hampden. The Hearts player was in deep trouble with Erchie.

'But ref, if you send me aff we'll probably no' win the cup, and ah wis lookin' forward to a ride oan an open-top bus.'

'In that case you'll jist need to go back tae Edinburgh an' get oan wan o' they tourist buses. Aff!'

'But, ref. He's been fouling me since the game started. Fur a minute ah jist saw red,' complained the Hibs captain.

'Well, haud oan another minute an' ah'll show you another shade o' red,' smiled Erchie, holding his red card aloft.

'Hey, ref. It wisnae me. He banjoed me,' said the scowling Cowdenbeath midfielder.

'Aye, well ye do seem a bit oot o' tune today, sunshine. Aff!'

'Right, that's enough of your persistent fouling, my friend,' Erchie said to the Aberdeen striker. 'You've got yerself a red card.'

'An' you know what ye can dae wi' yer red card, ref. Ye can stick it where the sun don't shine.'

'Too late, son. There's hunners up there already!' retorted Erchie. 'Aff!'

Erchie blew his whistle and went over to the Hibs defender who stood next to the goalpost, hands arrogantly on hips. 'Ye've been whistling on me aw day fur fouls, ref. Is that the only tune you can play on that wee whistle o' yours?' he asked sarcastically.

'How about ah play you Johnny Cash's 'Walk the Line' as you walk round the touchline and off the pitch? Aff!'

'Right,' Erchie said to the St Mirren striker. 'Ah'm sending you off.'

'What for?'

'The rest of the match, stupid!'

The Dumbarton midfielder was already on a yellow when he blatantly held the jersey of the East Fire striker who was through on goal.

'Right,' said Erchie. 'What's yer name?'

The player smirked and said, 'Simon Cowell.'

'Well, Mister Cowell, Britain may have talent but you sure don't. Aff!'

Managers

'Pittodrie's sodden, ref,' protested the Aberdeen manager. 'Ye surely cannae ask ma lads tae play the second half?'

The problem with your team is that they are so old they've dribbled all over the pitch in the first-half!'

'Congratulations, Gordon, on your appointment,' said Erchie to the new Dumbarton coach. 'Am I correct in thinkin' you started off life as an apprentice butcher?'

'Aye, ah did, Erchie.'

'Good. Because you might just be able tae do something with that pile o' mince you've inherited.'

It was half-time and Erchie was accosted by the St Johnstone manager.

'Ref, you're victimising me and ma boys. Ah'm gonnae write tae the SPFL aboot ye.'

'Well, ah hope yer spelling is better than their tackling,' observed Erchie.

The East Fife manager accosted Erchie at full-time. 'You sent off ma best player for foul and abusive language. He swears he didn't say a word.'

'He would swear that,' replied Erchie. 'Believe me that lad could make whole sentences out of sweary words.'

It was after the game, and the Aberdeen manager was protesting to Erchie about a sending off. 'Listen, Erchie, the lad wasn't fouling. He was just selling the centre back a dummy.'

'Aye, an' if ah were you ah would be thinking of selling a few dummies as well!'

'We're a team in transition, Erchie,' the Annan Athletic coach confided to the referee.

'Aye, ah can see that. Yer goin' fae bad tae worse.'

'I've installed new dietary rules since I took over this club,' said the Partick Thistle manager to Erchie. 'For instance I've changed the pre-match meal from steak to fish.'

'Well, it's working. They certainly played like a bunch o' haddies the day.'

The manager of Kilmarnock was chatting to Erchie after the game.

'Good game, Erchie. Whit dae ye think of ma new wonder striker?'

'No' bad,' agreed Erchie. 'But ye must wonder when he's gonnae score.'

'Aw referee. Gie ma boys a break. We're trying tae get intae Europe next season,' pleaded the Dundee United manager.

'If you ask me the only way that lot wull get intae Europe is tae book a Thomas Cook holiday,' observed Erchie.

'Don't you think ma winger is deceptive, Erchie?' asked the Kilmarnock manager.

'Aye, he's slower than you think.'

When Erchie arrived at Cappielow Park for the match between Morton and Hamilton he was met by both managers. 'Listen, Erchie, the gemme's a bogey. As you can see it's bucketing. They get an awful lot o' rain here in Greenock. The pitch is afloat, so we've both agreed that the match should be postponed.'

'Uch, no. It's only a wee drizzle. In the whole o' ma career ah've never had a player drown yet!'

'Well, Erchie. that's us promoted,' smiled the Falkirk manager. 'Ah've told the chairman that ah'm confident we'll stay up in the Scottish Premier Division for at least four seasons.'

'Aye,' agreed Erchie. 'Spring, summer, autumn and winter.'

'How are ye keeping?' Erchie asked the Brechin City manager. 'Ah heard ye were ill.'

'Yer right, Erchie. The problem is ah've got a bad back.'

'Well, it's actually two bad backs ye've got,' replied Erchie. 'And your central defender is a bit dodgy, too.'

'What do you think of my new striker, Erchie?' asked the St Johnstone manager. 'Does he not remind you a wee bit of Andy Murray?'

'Ah don't think ah agree wi' you. After all, Andy Murray hits the net occasionally.'

Pride, Prejudice
and Penalties

THE POSTAGE STAMP, the eighth hole at Royal Troon's Old Course, has much in common with Scottish football referee, Big Erchie.

It is respected, tricky, small, and dauntingly tough. At one Open, an unfortunate German amateur took fifteen strokes, and even the great Tiger Woods scored a triple bogey six at this exhilarating seminal golf hole when he played the course in the 1997 Open Championship.

Players coming up the seventh fairway are always apprehensive of the par three, 114 yard challenge, looming ahead at the eighth. As was Erchie, when he and his golfing buddy, Gordon Weir, a member at Royal Troon, holed out on the seventh.

Gordon, otherwise known as Nebbie, was a fellow referee and well known for his competitive streak. With his outgoing nature Nebbie was a stranger to inhibition, something he had in common with Erchie. As a footballer he hadn't quite managed to break into the higher echelons, and had subsequently transferred his footballing ambitions to refereeing. Nebbie was tall, wore his years lightly, had a nose like a truffle hound, hence his nickname and, much to the chagrin of his follically-challenged friend, was forever combing his full head of long, lush hair.

'Right, Erchie,' said Nebbie, 'how about a wee wager at the Postage Stamp?'

'Sure, Nebbie. How about a fiver?'

'A fiver? What's the matter with twenty quid? Ur ye not up fur it, wee man?'

Erchie cast him a rueful sidelong glance. 'No bother,' he replied with less than wholehearted enthusiasm, knowing Nebbie usually proved to be the better golfer with an especially unerring eye at putting. Previous wagers against the shrewd Nebbie had proved to be a gloomy catalogue of failures, but Erchie's stubborn reservoirs of self-esteem wouldn't let him back down, although he knew his chances were probably bleak.

In the lead through the previous seven holes, Nebbie had the honour. The eighth tee is higher than the green, being built atop a sandy rise. The green itself is also elevated, cut out of the side of a mighty dune, the top of which rises ominously above the left hand side of the putting surface. His beautiful lofted nine iron shot landed softly and settled on the green, five feet to the right of the hole.

Nebbie turned and looked at Erchie with a slight smile on his face as if to say, follow that.

Erchie teed up his ball, took a practice swing and looked ahead, focusing on the shot in front of him. Beyond the Postage Stamp the Firth of Clyde shimmered brilliantly and Ailsa Craig and the mountains of Arran appeared backlit by the sun in ultramarine and crimson. He swung at the ball which rose perfectly straight and high at the pin, before being caught by a sudden gust of the prevailing westerly wind making it veer left, landing on the far tip of the green.

'Aye, you were a wee bit lucky to get on the green, Erchie,' pronounced his opponent. 'Bad luck with that bit of wind.'

Erchie didn't reply, merely remaining tight lipped, relieved that at least he was on the green, if only just. He still had a chance.

Erchie found his ball on the edge of the putting surface. He had indeed been lucky it had not rolled away.

A determined Erchie took his time with the putt, conscious of the wind pulling at his trouser legs. The putt was stroked to a satisfying five inches from the hole. At least it was a modicum of success and should prove a safe par three.

Now it was Nebbie's turn. Erchie crossed his fingers hoping that his opponent might fluff his shot from five feet. But Nebbie's putt was true, the ball dropping with agonising slowness into the cup with a satisfying clunk.

Never the one to hold back on his feelings, Nebbie did a little dance on the green, putter held high to the sky.

'Well done,' said Erchie, thinking, ya jammy b*****d!

It was in the bar later, as Erchie was handing over his twenty pound note that Nebbie observed. 'Aye, I must confess that the Postage Stamp is one of my favourite holes. A small target like that with notorious occasional swirls makes it jist the kind of challenge that ah thrive oan. Any time ye want to lose money, Erchie, just give me a shout and we'll play the Postage Stamp again.'

One of Erchie's footballing heroes, Sir Alex Ferguson, had it on record that the only type of player he signed were bad losers. Erchie liked that, for he had to acknowledge that he was a bad loser himself and his pride was hurt. By heavens, he would need to think of a way of beating Nebbie. Twenty quid was too much to lose on one bet. There was now only one thing on his mind. Revenge.

During the next few weeks, Erchie referred to the internet a number of times, examining the layout of the tricky Postage Stamp, and working out how best to play the hole in stubborn pursuit of getting his money back.

At his local golf course in Glasgow, he asked the pro for a lesson, concentrating on short par three holes subject to wind. The pro also gave him some advice on the Postage Stamp. 'It's simple, really, Erchie. Only play it on a day when there is no wind.' And how many days in the year would that be? thought Erchie.

It was not long after these pro lessons that Nebbie phoned Erchie. 'Hey, wee man. How dae ye fancy yer chances down in Troon? Surely this time ye will make a better job of the Postage Stamp? What do you say?'

Erchie pondered for a moment as he sifted through the memory of the previous occasion. Was he ready to have another go at the unpredictability of the eighth hole? Mind you, he did like a challenge.

'No bother, Nebbie, when are you free?'

As they were both free of refereeing commitments the

97

following Sunday and a tee-off time was available, the match was duly arranged.

On the day there were a number of clouds in the sky but the forecast was high pressure and no rain. However, the seemingly ever-present westerly wind was blowing across the course.

Erchie was delighted to find he was playing well and mentally thanked his home professional for all his advice. When they came to the eighth the match was all square. Erchie was feeling surprisingly confident. And he was the one who would drive first.

'Right, Erchie, I assume we are playing for another twenty quid?'

Erchie looked ahead at the small target. Surely he could land the ball very near to the hole this time. 'How about double or quits, Nebbie? Let's call it forty.'

'Heavens above, wee man, you are in a bolshie frame of mind today. Fine, if you want to drop another forty notes then I'm on. Let's see if you're up to it.'

Selecting a wedge Erchie had a few swings. He looked around. Yes, the wind was blowing gently but seemed to be behaving itself today. He adjusted his feet a couple of times before hitting a high ball which landed plumb in the middle of the green. A lovely shot.

'Have you been practising?' asked Nebbie accusingly. 'Looks like I'm going to have my work cut out here.'

Nebbie's shot followed a similar path to Erchie's, landing just a foot away from Erchie's ball, some eight feet from the hole. It would now be a putting contest.

It was just clear that Nebbie's ball was probably a couple of inches further away from the hole so it would be his honour to play first.

Nebbie took his time lining up the putt. It looked relatively straightforward and it was. The ball rolled straight into the hole. Nebbie looked at Erchie, smirked, but said nothing.

The pressure was now on Erchie. He had carefully noted the route taken by Nebbie's ball. Erchie's putt rolled tantalisingly slowly towards the hole, seemed to wobble slightly as it hit the lip of the cup, then dropped. Both players had got birdies.

'Well done, wee man,' said Nebbie. 'For a moment there I thought I was going to get forty quid. Pity.'

'Ah'll get ma money back one of these days,' replied Erchie with some feeling. He was pleased he had played so well at this notoriously difficult hole but his ambition to at least get his money back was, for the meantime, thwarted.

It was a few weeks later when Erchie was refereeing at a League Two ground that he came across an idea. This particular club ran a scheme for supporters whereby the winners of their lucky ticket could enter a penalty-shootout competition. The reserve goalkeeper would troop out at half-time and face three penalties from each of the winners. The one who scored most penalties won twenty-five pounds. Maybe this could be a way of getting his money back from Nebbie. After all, he rationalised, they were both in the football business.

Would Nebbie fancy having wager on a contest like that? Could he beat him? He would think about it.

It was shortly after this that Erchie seemed to go through a period of misfortune. Firstly, he was caught speeding. He had been refereeing a match in Perth between St Johnstone and Celtic. On his way back to Glasgow on the busy A9, with its steady stream of supporters' buses and cars heading back to the city, his mind had been still on the game and his speed on the whizzing Harley gradually crept up. Suddenly he had become aware of a blue light flashing behind and a police car indicating for him to stop.

As two policemen came up to him he removed his helmet. 'Ye gods,' exclaimed one of them, a tall thin officer with deep-set and darting eyes combined with a sharp boned nose. 'Look who we've caught. It's Big Erchie himself.'

'So it is,' laughed the other policeman. 'Bit of a speed merchant today, Erchie, eh?'

'Was ah going too fast, officer?' asked Erchie innocently.

'Fast! One hundred and nine miles an hour on a sixty-mile-an-hour road. I'm going to have to get my red card out for that, Erchie.'

'But let me ask ye, boys. How come you've stopped me?' asked Erchie with a measure of caution. 'There are quite a few guys roaring down the road today.'

'I don't really know who reported you but somebody certainly did. From what I hear, you denied Celtic a stonewall penalty today and they only drew with Saints. This road is full of Celtic supporters with mobiles. It doesn't take a genius to work out that it could be payback time by various Celtic guys. You must know, Erchie, you're quite well known for scooting around Scotland on this motorbike of yours.'

The policeman probably had it bang on, realised Erchie. Most unfair, as it had never been a penalty in a million years.

'Don't tell me you two are football fans, too?' he asked.

The policemen grinned at each other. 'I'll deny saying this, Erchie, but we're Celtic fans.'

'Okay, boys. Enjoy yerselves. Book me.'

'We are booking you, Erchie, don't worry. Best catch we've had all year.'

Just then a number of supporters buses roared passed, grinning faces making rude signs from the windows.

'Well, looks like you're making some folks happy today,' observed Erchie with a sardonic smile.

Erchie was formally charged. Then, keen to get away from the passing gawping, jeering fans and their lusty unsophisticated singing, he quickly mounted his motorbike and continued on his way south – this time ensuring he didn't go over the designated speed limit!

Two nights later Erchie awoke with a raging toothache. No amount of paracetamol or whisky provided relief. As a result he had no option but to book an emergency appointment with his dentist, something he always dreaded.

On the way to the dentist's surgery the following day, he was plagued with recurrent memories of dental torture as a child. Following a fall from a haystack at the family farm he had broken three teeth. The resulting treatment had seemed equivalent to the thumbscrew. Thereafter he had an enduring fear of dental visits.

A masked Christopher Gilford BDS, a Highlander from Inverness now living in Glasgow, advanced upon Erchie, and plunged his anaesthetising syringe of lidocaine into the referee's gums, causing Erchie to jump. Soon the blocking numbness ceased any sensation, although this did not stop him mentally cursing those people who continually said modern dentistry was pain free.

'Now, now, Mister Smith,' came the muffled voice of the dentist, 'you're a man who is used to giving out suffering to football teams and fans, so what is a little pain to someone like you?'

Trying to keep his mouth open while exchanging small talk with Mister Gilford, was not easy, especially with a tongue apparently expanded to a balloon. The dentist prattled on about Scottish football through the continual whine of the drill, giving no opportunity for Erchie to respond. Finally the noise finished, Erchie spat out, wiping his dribbling chin and swirling the blood out of his mouth, before looking up anxiously at Mister Gilford for some good news. It was not forthcoming.

'Sorry, Erchie but I think this tooth can't be saved. I don't like doing extractions but we really have no option here. The decay is down to the root.'

Erchie's heart sank. More discomfort. The dental assistant duly supplied a new paper bib and Mr Gilford set off on his next task of extracting the tooth. It proved a lengthy job. First of all there was a snap as it broke and then came the job of digging out the root. Finally, Mister Gilford triumphantly held up the culprit and grinned. Erchie mentally sighed with relief before raising his wrist and looking at his watch. He had been in the chair for fifty minutes. The rack would have been easier.

As Mister Gilford tidied up in Erchie's mouth he observed, 'As a St Johnstone man myself I thought you handled our last match against Celtic well. Though you did miss a penalty we should have had.'

Erchie looked at him carefully while chewing a stoical rubber lip, incapable at that moment to reply. For heaven's sake you just can't win, can you, as a referee, he thought. The doubters and the bigots are ever alert for some slip-up which impacts their team. Then he wondered about the dentist's treatment of his teeth. Could there have been a bit of retribution today by this St Johnstone supporter? Grateful that his ordeal was finally over, he wearily got out of the chair.

It was around this time that the summons for speeding on the A9 arrived. It gave him the option of being fined four hundred pounds and three speeding points, or appealing and appearing in court. Erchie decided to pay while pondering whether it was time to move on from two wheels to four wheels. After all, he had driven a tractor around the farm in his youth so surely learning to drive a car would be easy. Decisively, he booked some lessons.

It proved not to be as easy as he had first thought. After a jerky first lesson, driving through the hinterland of Bearsden with instructor Mr Silverman, he realised there was a lot to learn. Indeed Mr Silverman's timely thumps on the dual controls was the only reason a couple of cyclists had remained on their bikes.

When it came to three point turns Erchie was forever forgetting to look in the mirror and apply the handbrake. He could see the instructor was not amused. This situation did not improve when a row of red traffic cones were bowled over like skittles and Erchie had lightly remarked there were too many on the roads, anyway. Mr Silverman wasn't pleased, especially when he later inspected the scrapes on the side of the car.

'We have got to get you to a much higher standard, Mr Smith. Otherwise the examiner will not be impressed.'

Erchie decided he would make a big effort to meet the standards required. He studied the Highway Code with the same zeal he had applied to the Referees' Handbook and FIFA's Laws of the Game. As a result he easily passed the Driving Theory Test.

Delighted, he applied for his driving test, despite Mr Silverman seeming unsure as to whether he was ready.

The test took place at Glasgow's Anniesland Testing Centre, not far from Erchie's home. He was quite confident as he knew all of the roads in the vicinity well. It was only afterwards, when the examiner was

writing out the fail slip and going over the points on
which he hadn't come up to standard that it sunk in.
Mr Silverman had been right. He clearly required further
lessons. As the examiner closed his clipboard book and
made to open the door of the car, he turned to Erchie
and with a determined look commented, 'By the way,
Mr Smith, or rather Big Erchie, the Gers' centre forward
Beattie wisnae offside in the recent Old Firm game.
That goal should've stood.' And with that he exited the
car, slamming the door.

Erchie sat for a minute in disbelief. It was mind-
boggling. Fur heaven's sake, he thought, am ah being
pilloried for being a ref? Then he remembered that his
mother always used to say that bad things happened in
threes, so at least that was the worst over.

His mother was wrong.

The following week Erchie was in London for two
days, having been invited to referee a charity match
between Arsenal and Crystal Palace. It was on the flight
back that he once more ran into a bit of a problem.

It was the last flight of the day from Heathrow to
Glasgow, and Erchie found himself in a middle seat
with two overweight guys on either side. From the
aroma wafting his way, Erchie came to the conclusion
they had both been at the sauce before boarding. The
one in the aisle seat seemed to be half asleep, contentedly
belching while his head lolled against the referee. The
massive arm of the dozing fellow at the window seat
overflowed onto the armrest leaving Erchie little room

to read his newpaper. Good job it's only a fifty minute flight, thought Erchie.

What he really felt like was a drink. Just one as he would be steering the Harley home from the airport. Might need to have my whisky intravenously, he thought. Doubt if I could get my meal table down with this pair beside me.

At the noise of clinking bottles and glasses on the trolley, both his fellow travellers miraculously revived, sitting up in anticipation.

The two guys ordered three vodkas each. Erchie contented himself with coffee and a whisky. But just as all three were taking their first sips the plane hit turbulence. It was the worst Erchie had experienced in all of his travels. The contents of his coffee cup seemed to miraculously rise from the cup and splash simultaneously in two directions, over the trousers of his two fellow passengers.

'Hey, whit the...!' they exclaimed in unison.

'Sorry, lads, couldn't be helped.'

As if in retaliation, the contents of one of their open vodka bottles flew over Erchie as the plane gave a frightening lurch.

'Wur gonnae die,' moaned the man on the aisle seat, suddenly holding onto Erchie's arm with the grip of a boa constrictor.

'Should've got the train,' proclaimed the other white-faced passenger.

It was at this very moment that the plane decided to

drop a thousand feet or so. Screaming came from all parts of the plane, including Erchie's companions.

The guy on Erchie's right suddenly proclaimed, 'Oh, God, just let me live long enough tae see Partick win the European Champions Cup.'

'You couldnae live that long!' countered the other fellow, while at the same time stretching for his sick bag.

Erchie couldn't help himself. 'Well, if they got rich owners who were prepared tae put money intae the team, buy eleven new players, then ye never know.'

Both guys looked at Erchie. 'Oh, ur you an expert, then? Listen, ah've been a fitba fan aw ma life an' Partick are aye up an' doon the leagues like the proverbial hoor's knickers. Nae consistency, that's their problem.'

Erchie could see that both his companions were now somewhat agitated. The alcohol, his spilt coffee, the bad turbulence, and now the mention of football, had got them steamed up. He decided to say nothing further and try to read his paper.

'Did ye no' hear me askin' you a question, pal! Ur you a fitba expert?'

Upon hearing the word 'pal', Erchie knew he could be in trouble. The rest of the flight would be tortuous. He opted for civility, the only answer in this tight situation.

'Sorry. Ah'm not an expert but ah do like ma football,' he replied.

'So ur you a Tim or a Blue-Nose?'

'Ah don't support any particular team... just the Scottish team.'

For a moment Erchie's attention was distracted by a passenger making his way along the aisle. The man, in a smart business suit, looked carefully at the referee and his fellow passengers, though his gaze lingered on Erchie, apparently trying to figure out who he was.

'But ur ye for Rangers or Celtic, that's whit ah want tae know?' asked the irate passenger on the aisle seat, displaying a worrying look of simmering discontent.

Erchie deliberated. An incident on an aircraft would be meat and drink to sports journalists, who would surely lampoon him in their columns full of rich withering irony.

Just then the businessman returned, stopped, and addressed himself to Erchie. 'Ah've been trying to place you. Ah said to masel, ah know that face. It's you, isn't it?'

Erchie almost came back with a quip but felt in the circumstances, with his uptight travelling companions beside him, it was more appropriate to merely nod. He sat awaiting the dreaded pronouncement of his identity.

'Aye, you were on the telly last Sunday on *Songs of Praise*. Ah knew ah recognised you,' pronounced the stranger.

Erchie looked at him in disbelief. Did he have some religious doppelganger?

Shocked, he smiled and nodded again at the man.

As the passenger moved away both his fellow travellers suddenly looked at him in a different light. With this pronouncement on his apparent religious fame their attitudes had clearly changed.

'Here, have a tissue to wipe yersell,' said the one on the aisle seat. 'Sorry if there wis a wee bit o' misunderstandin' there.'

'No problem,'

'Wid ye like a wee swally o' ma vodka? Ah've still got some left,' asked the fellow with the window seat.

'Eh, no thanks,' replied Erchie.

Thankfully the plane started its descent into Glasgow Airport and conversation ceased. The last minutes of flight remained peaceful and before they disembarked the aircraft both men shook Erchie's hand.

A much relieved Erchie made his way to the baggage pick-up point. As he watched the moving carousel for his bag he felt a tap on the shoulder. It was the *Songs of Praise* viewer.

'Oh, nice to see you again,' said Erchie politely.

'Ah could see you had a bit of an interesting situation going on there in the plane,' the stranger said. 'So let me tell you. I want at least three penalties fur St Mirren the next time you're refereeing, Erchie. You owe me!' The fellow slapped Erchie on the back and moved off.

Erchie was taken aback. Well, right enough, ah do owe ye one, pal, he thought. Quick witted football fan that.

In the following weeks nothing further untoward occurred to disturb Erchie's life. And so once more his thoughts turned to getting some payback from Nebbie. The twenty quid he had lost on the Postage Stamp hole at Troon still rankled. He had been railroaded into it by Nebbie who knew fine he could never turn down a wager.

So what about a penalty shoot-out? It could be fun. Would he win? Could he outfox Nebbie? They were both involved in soccer so he would talk to Nebbie about it. Anyway, he argued, a goal was really just a larger postage stamp. He decided to phone Nebbie.

'Hi Nebbie, how's it going?'

'Fine, Erchie. I was actually just thinking about you. Is it not time for us to have another wee go at your favourite golf hole down in Troon. I hope you're not going to chicken out, now? What do you say?'

'Well, actually ah wis thinkin' something along a different line, Nebbie. At a League Two match some weeks back they had a penalty shoot-out contest at half time, ye know, for the punters. How do you fancy your chances at penalties, Nebbie? We could get a goalie and let's say we each take five penalties, and see who can score most goals.'

'Forget the goalie idea, Erchie. Let's just make it that we try to score penalties against each other.'

'You mean we take it in turns being in goal?'

'Exactly.'

Erchie hesitated. He hadn't thought of doing it this way. For goodness sake, he was probably five inches shorter than Nebbie. But after all he had suggested the idea so he could hardly back out.

'Fine, Nebbie. Why don't we meet up for a drink and discuss the rules?'

A couple of evenings later the duo met to arrange the contest and agree the rules. Five penalties each was what it would be. If the score was equal after this then it would be sudden death. A wager of fifty pounds was agreed. This meant that if Erchie won he would have got his money back, plus thirty pounds. If Nebbie won he would be up seventy pounds. Erchie couldn't possibly allow that. He would need to practice. They had both agreed that one of their fellow referees would oversee the contest which would no doubt mean the whole of the refereeing fraternity would learn of it. Nebbie volunteered to arrange for the contest to take place one Sunday morning at Lesser Hampden.

In the local playing fields adjacent to his home, Erchie had a few practice sessions with a friendly neighbour who had played football at Junior level. It was just as he had thought. When it came to taking a penalty he was pretty consistent. His technique of applying the boot and hitting the ball as hard as possible seemed the best option for him.

However, when it came to playing goalkeeper, he was at a distinct disadvantage. Shots within his reach were fine but those hit towards the corners of the goal were difficult to get to.

Nearby some boys had been having a kickabout and when they saw penalties being taken they came over and asked if they could have a go. Most of their shots also whizzed past Erchie. Perhaps ah would have been better opting for the Postage Stamp again, he thought.

One wee lad seemed to be particularly adept, scoring with all of his penalties. Eventually as the boys were moving off the wee lad approached Erchie. 'Dae ye want some advice, mister?'

'Ah could certainly do with it,' Erchie replied, downcast.

'Well, ye see what ye are doin' is yer guessin' where the ball is gonnae go. Ye jist dive tae wan side or the other. That's nae good. You've got tae look at the fellow's eyes. That'll tell ye where he is gonnae place it. It fairly bamboozles them.'

'Right, son. Thanks fur the tip,' said Erchie.

When Erchie's neighbour resumed his penalty takings the referee decided to try out the wee fellow's advice. After a number of penalties Erchie concluded that it was not a perfect method, but certainly more successful than his hitherto strategy of just guessing.

And so the morning of the contest dawned. Grey clouds scurried across the sky and the BBC forecast gales later on in the day with the possibility of some of Scotland's bridges being closed to high-sided vehicles. Perhaps not the best weather conditions for a penalty competition, Erchie thought.

In the shadow of its nearby big brother, Lesser Hampden was still a smart looking small football ground. The synthetic pitch of third generation astro-grass was in good condition and Nebbie had said he would arrange for a net to be put up on one of the goals, ready for the day's proceedings.

As Erchie drove to Lesser Hamden he was filled with trepidation. His nerves were not helped by the increasing gusts of wind which hit the heavy Harley with its low centre of gravity, causing him to be extra careful when he had to slow down.

As Erchie arrived at the ground he was met by Nebbie and veteran referee Sammy McGill, a friend of both of them, who would oversee the contest. 'Ah've brought ma notebook and ma cards with me so ah hope ah don't have to send any of you two off today,' he joked.

Entering the ground Erchie immediately saw there were at least a dozen people standing behind the designated goal. One of them Erchie recognised as a journalist. 'Hey, Nebbie, ah thought this was a private competition?'

Nebbie grinned, winked and replied. 'Well, ye can't help it if word gets around, can you?'

By crivvens, thought Erchie, Nebbie must really fancy his chances today.

They then went to the dressing rooms to get kitted out before making their way on to the pitch to the accompaniment of some cheers from the phalanx of spectators. Erchie was then taken aback as suddenly from the loudspeaker system came the theme tune from *Gladiator*.

Nebbie turned, laughed and said. 'Thought I would just instil a wee bit of atmosphere, Erchie.'

Erchie had a sense today was not going to turn out as he had hoped.

'Okay, boys,' instructed Sammy, 'have a few practice hits and then we'll get going.'

Both men duly blasted a few shots into the empty net.

'Right,' said Sammy. 'We'll toss for who goes first. You shout, Erchie.'

'Heads,' said Erchie. The coin bounced once on the artificial surface and came up tails.

'Okay, then, I'll take the first penalty,' said Nebbie confidently.

Erchie put on the goalkeeper's gloves he had borrowed and stood on the goal line, arms in the air.

Nebbie took a long run up and hit the ball past past Erchie's left hand side.

'Okay, wee man. Your turn,' smiled the jubilant Nebbie.

Erchie placed the ball carefully on the penalty spot. Took a few steps back only to see the wind hit the ball which rolled away. Quickly recovering the ball he stuck it firmly on the spot before hitting it quickly in case it rolled away again. Big mistake. The ball flew into the waiting arms of Nebbie.

A determined Erchie once more donned the goalkeeping position. He remembered the advice given to him by the wee lad; watch the eyes of the penalty taker. Accordingly he stared at Nebbie's eyes. Nebbie again took a long run, glanced to Erchie's left side and hit the ball viciously in that direction. It was a futile effort, as Erchie had already launched himself in that direction, wrapping his gloves securely around the ball in mid-air.

Erchie was pleased. For his turn Erchie waited until

a gust of wind passed before setting down the ball. He took his time, decided where he was going to put it and stroked the ball into Nebbie's right had corner. One each after two penalties. He was still in with a chance.

After four penalties apiece the score was just two each. The wind had played havoc with the ball.

'It's penalty number five, boys,' Sammy announced unnecessarily. 'This could be decisive. If not we go into sudden death.'

Nebbie had lost his exuberant mood. This was serious now. He carefully placed the ball and strode back for his long run. Erchie watched his eyes. A few steps off the ball his eyes darted left. At the same time a tremendous gust of wind blew his long thick hair across his face and the shot sailed over the bar.

'Sammy! Ah need tae take this again. The wind blinded me.'

'What he needs is a haircut, Sammy,' said Erchie. 'Not another kick. I've never ever seen anybody get another penalty kick because their hair was too long.'

'It's all right for you, Erchie,' moaned Nebbie. 'You're getting a bit short in that department.'

'Every cloud has a silver lining,' Erchie philosophised.

Nebbie was less than pleased but took up his position on the goal line. In an effort to wind up Erchie he shouted, 'You're going to miss this time, wee man. This swirling wind is just like the Postage Stamp, eh? You've just been lucky so far.'

Erchie was calm. This was his big opportunity. As

he placed the ball on the spot he glanced at the intense figure of Nebbie staring directly at the ball and decided not to try to place the ball, but just hit it. The kick went straight at the centre of the goal. Nebbie had no chance as he had dived to the right. Goal! Erchie had won.

In the dressing room a downcast Nebbie reluctantly handed over the cash. He grumbled, 'You do appreciate, Erchie, that if the bet had been at the Postage Stamp I would have won.'

'Is that so, Nebbie?' replied a jubilant Erchie. 'Well, today demonstrates that fitba can lick a Postage Stamp!'

Throw-Ins

'Referee, you're jist card-happy,' quipped the mischievous Dumbarton striker.

'Too true. Ah'll tell ye when ma birthday is an' ye can send me wan.'

'Referee, ah don't think we see eye tae eye on your decisions,' moaned the Ayr United midfielder.

'Yer right, big man. Ah'm five feet five and you're over six feet. But ony mair o' yer lip an' ah'll soon cut you doon tae size,' retorted Erchie.

'Stop niggling me, sonny,' shouted Erchie to the cheeky Livingston winger.

'But ye'r blind, ref. That wis a blatant hand ball. Ye should've gone tae Specsavers!'

'They phoned me jist afore the game but ah didnae have time tae collect ma new specs!'

'Heads or tails?' Erchie asked the Dunfermline Athletic captain.

'Heads, ah feel lucky,' came the reply. 'Ah won ten pounds on the lottery last week.'

'Well it's tails, so if ah were you ah widnae buy ony tickets this week!'

'You're making a right meal o' refereeing the game today, referee,' complained the Partick Thistle captain.

'Listen, sunshine. All you've done today is moan. Fur heaven's sake try McDonalds on yer way home an' get yerself a Happy Meal!'

'Hey, Ref! That's less than ten yards fur this free kick,' protested the Partick Thistle defender. 'Ah widnae like you tae measure curtains fur ma wife.'

'Only more o' yer patter an' it'll be curtains fur you, sunshine.'

'Listen, referee. Ah think you're pickin' oan me cause ah'm Celtic's best striker. Ah'll have you know lots of people clap when they see me.'

'Aye, Rangers fans wi' their hands clapped over their eyes!'

'Whit kind o' a call was that, referee, I ask you? You were miles away fae me when ah tackled him,' protested the Cally midfielder.

'I'm jist lookin after your health, sonny. To me you're looking a bit yellow, maybe jaundice, eh? Soon ye might be seeing red before your eyes. So watch it!' warned Erchie.

Goal Of The Month?

ALL ROADS SEEMED TO LEAD TO HAMPDEN. The surrounding streets and car parks swarmed with supporters proudly displaying their team colours. Nearby, buses, cars and taxis were decorated with brightly-coloured streamers.

Fans converged on the national stadium. Stewards checking everyone had a ticket.

Hampden was full; emotional frisson permeated the occasion. All 52,000 seats were occupied. Live coverage of the match on television. It had been an arduous route to the final for both teams and now an all-out battle was expected.

At one end of the stadium a massive swathe of green scarves waved in unison as the Hibees' fans anticipated their heroes.

At the other end, wearing maroon regalia, were Hearts' supporters contributing to the racket for this derby cup final.

Both sets of fans feverishly cheered as Erchie and his assistant referees led the teams out onto the lush green turf. The roar was deafening. Each player held the hand of a youngster dressed in their club's colours. Then the teams lined up to be introduced to various dignitaries, including Scotland's First Minister.

The watery sunshine shone on the sparkling green of the famous old playing surface. Above the stadium a skein of pigeons appeared, no doubt frightened by the loud machinations of the crowd.

The coin toss was duly won by Hibs, who opted to play with the majority of their supporters behind them, on the east terracing.

Amidst a hubbub of anticipation both teams nervously started the match, then Hibs began to set the pace. They started to dominate the exchanges with some wonderful moves, ending up in a number of near misses on the Hearts goal. Hibs' mercurial left winger was giving the Hearts defence a torrid time, and it was inevitable, when he once more beat off a few last minute desperate tackles, that Hibs would score. He slipped the ball inside for the striker leading the Hibs attack who opened his feet and simply passed the ball into the corner of the net.

The ocean of Hibs supporters exploded. 'Gooaall!' they shouted. Scarves waved in unison as they sang and screamed their pleasure.

The teams lined up once more. Although Hearts were now having more of the ball, the play was still predominately with Hibs. Then the hardworking Hearts' midfielder, a tenacious box-to-box player, put a long ball through the middle, allowing their lurking central striker to round the Hibs keeper and equalise. The Hearts fans jumped for joy. Up until that moment it had appeared as though the game could be slipping away from them.

It was at this stage in the match that Erchie could tell things were changing. He liked to keep the game flowing and entertaining, especially in a Cup Final, but a few tackles were now flying in, with the Hibs target man in particular laying it about a bit.

Erchie ran up beside him, 'Listen, sunshine,' Erchie warned. 'I don't mind players having a competitive streak but there are only three players at this Cup Final today giving me grief, and you're the not-so-good, the bad and the ugly… in other words, all of them. You can't go around kicking players the way you do, otherwise ah wid need tae find out who their next-of-kin is. So watch it!'

Surprisingly at half-time the score remained tied with both sets of fans having much to discuss over their Bovril. But this situation was not to last long. Ten minutes into the second half the Hibs winger again danced through Hearts' midfield-line unchallenged, nutmegged their right full-back before coolly slotting the ball past an exposed keeper. A superb move and strike.

The Hibs end of Hampden duly went into a state of ecstasy, lifting the decibel level to new heights.

After this the outlook started to look bleak for Hearts. The intensity of the game was increasing with the Hibees setting the pace, but tackles were still over aggressive and it was starting to get somewhat 'tasty'. Hibs' target man was again a culprit and, after a number of bad fouls, Erchie was forced to halt play.

'Listen, sonny,' Erchie told the player with growing exasperation. 'You're now on a yellow. Behave or yer manager will substitute you in case you get a red. Ah bet there are subs on your bench that wid chop their legs aff to get a game in this final.'

With fifteen minutes to go the match turned on its head, Hibs' target man latched onto a long ball in the box and turned for goal, chased by one of the Hearts central defenders. Suddenly the Hibs player fell head-over-heels to the ground, rising quickly with his arms outstretched appealing for a penalty. The Hibs fans rose in unison claiming a spot kick.

Erchie stopped play and called the Hibs player over.

'Aw, r-e-f-e-r-e-e!' shouted the player, wide-eyed and feigning ignorance, spittle forming at his mouth like a rabid dog, 'Don't tell me you jist give us fouls that are ootside the box? That wis a blatant foul oan me inside the box.'

Erchie stonewalled him. 'Let me tell you something, sonny, that wis the best dive I've seen since ma school swimming gala,' before holding up a yellow card followed by a red. 'Two bookable offences. Aff!'

The Hibs fans went berserk. They hissed and booed, and their manager with obvious exasperation was seen raging against the assistant referee. Erchie, impervious to the uproar, ran over, told him to calm down, and sent him to the stand.

The furore continued, then intensified, as the Hearts team now became ever more confident against their ten-man opponents. A long, cross-field pass found the wingman on the right who cut inside and hit an unstoppable cannonball shot, which dropped under the crossbar into the net, despite the valiant attempt by the Hibs goalkeeper. The Hearts fans duly gave way to their delight with lusty unsophisticated singing.

The remaining few minutes were tense as extra time approached. Erchie looked at his watch. A minute to go. Just then, a desperate punt by a Hearts defender found his team's lone striker, who swiftly turned and hit a speculative thirty-yard drive. It struck the inside of the post. The goalkeeper was well beaten. The ball trundled along the goal line, bits of mud slowing its progress as it came to rest against the other post. A Hibs defender ran back and swiftly hit the ball into the outfield. Had it gone over the line? Erchie looked at the assistant referee waiting for some communication. It seemed to be an eternity before the voice in Erchie's earpiece said, 'Erchie, I think it was a goal.'

Erchie made a decision and gave the goal. Immediately he was surrounded by Hibs players protesting the decision. He held up his hand to stem the flow of dissenting voices.

Protestations also came from the Hibs supporters congregated behind the Hibs goal, but this quickly descended into shocked silence. The Jam Tarts fans couldn't believe their luck as immediately after the kick off Erchie blew for full-time.

Within minutes great swathes of Hibs fans had left the stadium, apart from some punters who continued to hurl threats and abuse at Erchie.

'There could be some fun after today's match, I'm

afraid, Erchie,' observed the assistant referee who had given the goal as the three officials trooped off together.

'It looked over the line to me,' mused Erchie, 'and you thought so, too, didn't you? Anyway, it was certainly an eventful ninety minutes.'

'Well, yes. I think it was over. Let's just keep our fingers crossed that the TV cameras agree with us, otherwise we really are in for stick. There'll be a number of people spitting blood.'

'We called it as we saw it,' said the indomitable Erchie. 'No regrets now, boys. A man with regrets is a man with weaknesses.'

Coming off the pitch Erchie was buttonholed by a het up Hibs manager, a dusting of stubble on his angrily clenched jaw. The manager locked eyes with Erchie. A red mist had clearly descended and the ranting language was colourful. Erchie opted to merely raise a red card in front of him.

Soon the irate Hibs captain led his downcast team up the centre stand stairs to receive their runners-up medals from the First Minister. Then the Hearts players were presented with their winners' medals and the cup to the loud acclaim of their supporters. Shortly afterwards the despondent Hibs team disappeared into the tunnel.

Erchie and his assistant referees then climbed the stairs to receive their medals. Following this, the jubilant Hearts team had their team photograph taken on the sponsor's rostrum in the middle of the park amid a shower of pyrotechnics, before running to the end of the stadium where their ecstatic fans waved and sang.

It was afterwards in the officials' changing room that the news was received. Television replays showed that the ball was not over the line. Furthermore, outside the door the Hibs manager and chairman were waiting for Erchie.

The chairman was the calmer of the two despite his florid complexion. 'Erchie, you've been very fair to us in the past. But today you robbed us of an important bit of silverware. You should have given us a cast-iron penalty, and then you went on to give a goal against us which was not a goal. You're losing your touch wee man!'

'First of all, it most certainly was not a penalty,' replied Erchie calmly. 'Anyway, I've not seen the TV replays. From my angle the ball appeared to be over the line, so it was a goal and that's what it will remain.'

Before the manager beside him could launch into another tirade of abuse he was dragged away by the chairman, now in danger of losing his control, 'I'll be reporting you to the Head of Referee Operations and the newspapers will be all over you. You're finished, Erchie, I hope you appreciate that!'

As the officials left the stadium, the assistant referee who had flagged the goal said, 'Sorry about that, Erchie.'

'Don't worry about it,' replied Erchie. 'We both called it as we saw it. That's all that we can do. It's all right for those refs in the English Premier Division who have technical support like Hawkeye, but we just have to do our best. Anyway,' he philosophised, 'it gives the fans and the sports journalists something to moan about. Never mind lads, ah'm away. See you later.' And with that, Erchie went to collect his motorbike, parked only yards away in Hampden's underground roadway.

As Erchie roared off through the car park he was berated by the crocodiles of Hibs fans, still radiating menace, as they boarded their buses. A volley of half-eaten pies were thrown in his direction which caused him to swerve.

Not one of my better days, thought Erchie as he carefully steered himself onto the M74 and made for home. Oh well, some you win and some you lose.

Back home he poured himself a large malt and settled down, not without some trepidation, to watch the recording of the final. May as well get this over, he thought.

As the recording progressed he mentally appraised each of his decisions and concluded they were correct. That was until he came to the ordering off incident when the Hibs player ostensibly dived in the box. The slow motion replays were inconclusive but the TV commentators thought that Erchie's decision was probably, on balance, correct. Thank heavens for that, muttered Erchie.

Then came the goal that never was. Here the cameras had unfortunately done a good job. It was obvious the ball hadn't gone over the line before being whipped away by the Hibs defender. 'Shit!' exclaimed Erchie. 'Ah really am in the shit.' No doubt the mistake would be replayed many times and magnified by both fans and media.

As he poured himself a further malt his mobile went off. It was the Head of Referee Operations. 'Erchie, have you watched the recording of the Final yet?'

'Fraid so, John. Looks like ah blew it.'

'Looks like it. Not good, Erchie, I've got to say. I've already had my ear blown off by the Hibs chairman. To say our discussion was acrimonious and inconclusive is an understatement. Told him that we are merely human and sometimes we get it wrong. Did the assistant referee agree with you on this one, Erchie?'

'Well, he did, John, but I must say that from my vantage point ah thought it was over the line. Obviously ah was wrong in this instance.'

'Right,' said the Head of Referee Operations, 'why don't you come in and see me next week once the dust has settled and we'll talk about it. Okay?'

'Sure,' replied Erchie, knowing that it would probably mean he would not be refereeing any finals in the immediate future.

The following day the newspapers crucified Erchie. 'We ain't got a Hawkeye, we've got a Birdseye Custard Pudding!' ran one headline. Various photographs showed the ball on the line, but not over it. It seemed they had gone to town with reams and columns dashed off on the story. Erchie gave the papers a quick scan then opted, with his usual devil-may-care gusto, not to wallow in the situation but to shrug it off.

The meeting with the Head of Referee Operations was to prove better than he expected. 'Erchie,' the boss began, 'we all know your reputation in the business, but this incident is big. A fundamental part of refereeing is consistency and you have been consistent over the years. Unfortunately now with television our mistakes are magnified to the whole world.'

'Listen,' said Erchie, 'ah have got tae haud up ma hands in this instance and admit it should never have been given as a goal. But there's no going back.'

'You're right, Erchie. I've made mistakes in my time, too,' admitted the Head of Refereeing Operations. 'Every referee has. We just have to ride the vicissitudes of criticism. But we get it right probably nine times out of ten. It's amazing, managers and coaches will stand up for their players no matter what they've done. And, if they can't defend them, they try and get away with the usual nonsense of temporary blindness by claiming they didn't see the incident. And as for supporters, they only know of two refereeing decision: those that go in favour of their team, and those that are wrong. The only good referee as far as they are concerned is a dead one.

'Unfortunately in this case the Hibs manager and fans are right. Anyway, the season is almost over. However, be assured, Erchie, in my eyes you're still the man for the big occasion. Personally I suspect you went with your assistant referee's decision and you didn't have a clear sighting, eh?'

'It's very simple, boss, the buck stops wi' me, as they say,' replied Erchie. 'Anyway, I always say that if matches flowed from end to end, if there was no feigning of injuries, no histrionics, no swearing, no diving, and all the players agreed amongst themselves what the decisions were, then there would be no need fur referees.'

'I don't think I'll live long enough to see that,' laughed the Head of Refereeing Operations.

At work Erchie had to suffer a number of gibes from his colleagues, but this was something he had to endure most weeks. This time they were a bit more pointed though, especially from the one Hibs fan in the office. Ah wish he would move back east, that one. Erchie laughed them off, as usual making sure he had the last word.

However a couple of the Scottish sports journalists continued to write soberingly critical articles on the 'goal that never was'. Erchie would have loved to reply to their observations but that would have been frowned upon by the SPFL.

His next game was at Cappielow, the ground of Greenock Morton. It was to be a top of the Championship tussle between the home team and Raith Rovers, their rivals for the league. Erchie was determined that all should go well and to re-establish his credibility.

For this match he had been allocated assistant referees Brody McAllister and James Sheridan. Brody he had worked with before and Erchie knew him as sharp, reliable individual whose calls were usually spot on. James Sheridan was a relatively inexperienced referee who had only recently come into the big time. Erchie just hoped he was up to it, as no doubt a few sports reporters would be scrutinising each and every decision made.

In the officials' changing room he briefed his two assistant referees. 'Listen, boys. You all know aboot the goal ah mistakenly gave at the cup final, so it is essential that you help me and get your decisions correct today. At least there are no TV cameras here at this match. Just don't lose your concentration and keep up with play at all times. Ah know you will be your professional selves.'

'Okay, Erchie. Don't worry. We'll stay alert,' replied Brody. James Sheridan merely nodded.

A steady drizzle had fallen all day, and perhaps impacted by the dismal conditions the first-half proved to be a dull and scrappy affair with both sides lacking composure. In the second-half the match settled down. It was obvious that both managers had made a few changes to their line-ups. The flow of play was entertaining and the hardy, damp crowd warmed to the action.

If anything, the home team were gaining ascendancy with the away team becoming somewhat sloppy in possession. Suddenly a loose clearance by the Raith goalkeeper allowed the Morton centre forward, a fleet-of-foot poacher, to pounce on the ball and snatch a goal.

Erchie blew for the goal and the teams lined up once more.

Raith, urged on by their coach bawling from the technical area, went all out for an equaliser. Both of Morton's centre backs were now under pressure from a newly inspired Raith Rovers. First of all, a thirty-five yard shot hit the bar and then only a terrific block by the Morton goalkeeper prevented an equaliser.

It was not surprising with all their attacking that Raith had a number of corner kicks. It was after one corner kick that Erchie heard James Sheridan's voice in his earpiece. 'Erchie, watch that Raith centre forward. When he thinks you're not looking he stands on the goalkeeper's toes.'

'Thanks, James. Ah'll keep ma eye on him.'

With only a few minutes to play Erchie awarded Raith another corner. As the ball came over Erchie saw that the centre forward was indeed standing on the frustrated Morton goalkeeper's toes. At the very last minute the centre forward sprung into action, stepped off the goalie's feet and back-heeled the ball into the net.

Erchie blew his whistle for a foul. Suddenly the Raith players were all over him like a rash protesting that the goal had been legitimate. He calmly shooed them off before calling the Raith striker over. 'Ur you trying tae go up in the world, son, standin' on other folk's toes? That's a yellow for you.'

The centre forward gave a cunning smile but didn't protest.

The match ended with Morton winning by the single goal. The first thing Erchie did in the dressing room was to thank Sheridan for his timely tip. 'Ah would probably have given that as a goal if you hadn't put me wise tae his tricks, so well spotted, James.'

The headline in the *Sunday Post* football report the following day was, 'First Class Game by Big Erchie.' The narrative then went on to state that Erchie had refereed the match extremely well with no trace of nerves following his cup final slip-up.

The following week Erchie was allocated the final game of the season. A reschedules league match between Hibs and Hearts at Easter Road. Erchie suspected that the Head of Refereeing Operations had deliberately arranged this so he could re-establish his reputation.

Both teams were mid-table and there was nothing to play for. The only bit of interest according to the *Edinburgh Evening News,* would be that Big Erchie was refereeing. Erchie was reasonably relaxed about the whole thing, although he knew he would probably receive a hot reception from the Hibs fans, especially in their own stadium.

The Edinburgh weather for this match proved to be windy and cool, with the possibility of some light rain. It was therefore surprising that the crowd was a few thousand larger than would reasonably have been expected for an end of the season affair. The officials with him were Brody McAllister and James Sheridan, the assistant referees at the recent Morton and Raith match. As they stripped off, Brody informed Erchie that the TV cameras were covering the match. 'Well, we'd better not slip up,' was Erchie's only reply.

As the officials made their way to the tunnel onto the pitch they encountered the sullen faces of the Hibs chairman and manager. The chairman even came over and whispered threateningly, 'As far as I'm concerned, you're drinking in the last-chance saloon, Erchie.'

'Okay, make mine a Glenmorangie, then,' smiled Erchie.

As Erchie walked out onto the park at the start, he was met by incessant booing from the Hibs fans. A number of banners had been prepared, making insulting comments about the referee, and these were waved every time he made a decision against the home team.

It proved to be a surprising and frenetic game with the players apparently aware that the result was important to the bragging rights of their fans. Opportunities came at both ends of the park for goals but both teams seemed intent on scorning them.

It was half-way through the second half when the incident occurred that would once more put Erchie into the headlines. The promised light rain and wind had materialised and the grass was getting slippy. Erchie had given a corner kick to Hibs. Their main striker went over to take the kick. When the ball came over, the Hearts keeper came out for it, jumping above the crowded melee of players. He opted to punch the ball, but only managed to knock it onto the shoulder of the nearby Erchie who hadn't seen it coming. The ball then bounced back towards the goal, hanging agonisingly in the air for a moment before hitting the underside of the bar and bouncing over the goal line.

Erchie looked in disbelief. He had inadvertently scored a goal.

Easter road was in an uproar. Although the Hearts players protested, Erchie had no option but to award the goal. The Hibs players were all smiles and the mood of their fans suddenly changed. Erchie's name was chanted, laughingly acclaiming his unfortunate contribution to the match.

That was to remain the final score.

After the match in the corridor leading to the official's dressing room Erchie was met by sarcastic smiles from the Hibs manager and chairman.

As he walked past them Erchie decided to get his retaliation in first. 'Won't get me the Golden Boot Award, guys, but might make Goal of the Month!'

'Maybe ah should've gone tae Specsavers, eh?'

Extra Time

'Aw naw! That's the third penalty in succession ah've hit over the goal,' wailed the Raith Rovers targetman.

'Maybe you should give up football, son, and work in a pub. You only seem tae be good at putting shots over a bar.'

The Rangers forward scuffed his shot from three yards, an absolute sitter. Embarrassed, he immediately pulled his shirt over his head, rolled up the legs of his shorts and raised his arms in the air in despair.

'Behave yerself,' ordered Erchie. 'Whit dae ye think this is, Comic Relief Day?'

'Not oor day, referee. Five nothing and it's only half-time,' moaned the Elgin City player as they all trudged off at Borough Briggs Park. 'It's a right muddy pitch and if we're not careful it could end up a cricket score.'

'Right enough,' agreed Erchie. 'You're certainly on a sticky wicket.

'R-e-f-e-r-e-e! When ah took that corner kick ah goat a lot o' coins thrown at me,' moaned the Rangers.

'How much?' asked Erchie.

'Aboot four pound odds.'

'The way your lot are playin' the day, son, that's the only bonus you'll be getting,' smiled Erchie.

'Ah wis only playing the day, referee, because otherwise ah wid need tae have taken the wife tae Tesco,' joked the Inverness Cally player as they all trooped off at Caledonian Stadium at full-time.

'If ah had been you, son, ah wid have gone shopping. At least at Tesco you might have got some points.'

'Ref! That defender keeps kickin' ma left foot an' ah'm a one-footed player,' moaned the Hibs winger.

'Stop moaning, sonny,' instructed Erchie. 'So wis Long John Silver an' he did okay.'

'Ref! Watch that defender o' Ross County.
He tackles dirty,' moaned the Dundee forward.
'Ah think he jist wants tae see how far ah can
limp'.

'Well, if you retaliate wance mair ye'll limp back tae
the dug out.'

'He deliberately kicked ma testicles, referee,'
moaned the Dundee United central defender,
his face white as he clutched his groin.

'Well, if it's any consolation, son,' replied Erchie,
'it's the first time today he's managed to make proper
contact with a ball.'

Erchie blew his whistle to stop play. 'Do you know what a football looks like, sonny?' he said threateningly to the Ross County striker.

'Of course, ref.'

'Well, would you mind kicking it then, rather than the other players?'

'Are you blind, ref?' moaned the Ayr United half-back.

'Aye, ah am, sonny. So in a minute you're going to have to write yer ain name in ma notebook. Ma appointment wi' Specsavers is no' till next month!'

It had been raining hard in Dundee, and it was touch and go whether or not the local derby march between Dundee and Dundee United would go ahead.

The toss of the coin was won by the Dundee United captain. 'Right,' asked Erchie, 'deep end or the shallow end?'

The Kilmarnock midfielder was being substituted, but didn't seem to be making any move to leave the field.

'Right, sunshine. You're being substituted,' said Erchie.

'Oh, ah didnae see the guy holding up the board.'

'Whit did ye think it wis,' asked Erchie. 'Bingo numbers?'

Two St Mirren players were chatting. 'Whit dae ye think o' that referee, Big Erchie? Lets ye away wi' nothing that one.'

'Yer right. Yon wisnae born. Yon wis quarried.'

'A streaker ran onto the field at Celtic Park just as a penalty was being taken by the Celtic captain. He slipped on his run up and the ball flew over the bar.

'It wis that naked wummin that pit me aff, referee,' he complained bitterly.

'Tough, son,' replied Erchie with a mischievous grin. 'But don't worry, if she's still around at full time ye might score then!'

A Short History of Refereeing

MOST FOOTBALL MATCHES in the early 19th century did not have a referee. However with the evolution of rules came the need for someone to interpret them.

Refereeing, or umpiring, of games way back in the 19th century could be difficult. There were only two officials, both located on the side-lines. In 1865, tape was first introduced between the goal posts but it was not until 1882 that it was compulsory to mark out the pitch boundary and the exact area in which goalkeepers could handle the ball. Indeed it was not until 1912 that handling of the ball by goalkeepers was restricted to the penalty area. Having said that, it was in 1887 that the 12 yard penalty line arrived and a penalty could finally be awarded for fouls in this area. In 1887 the centre circle also came about, forcing the opposition to keep their distance at kick offs. In 1891, 12 and 18 yard lines were introduced across the breadth of the pitch, the former marking the area in which a penalty could be awarded. In 1902, the 18 yard line became the penalty box as we know it today. It was not until 1937 that the 'D' curve was added just outside the box, behind which all players must stand when a penalty is being taken.

The early umpires were usually non-playing members

of the football clubs involved. They would wave white handkerchiefs to indicate an offence. A third official was added towards the end of the 1870s in order to make a final decision when the two umpires disagreed. This third official soon earned the title of 'referee'. In 1891 the referee was finally decreed to be in overall charge of the match and was deemed mandatory for any game. Funnily enough, at that time the team captains drew the referee's attention to an infringement rather than the referee taking the initiative. Full power was given to referees in 1898 when neutral linesmen replaced club umpires.

Referees now use a pea whistle to indicate the start or restart of play, to delay play due to an infringement or injury, and to indicate the end of each half of the game.

Up until the 1950s, referees wore blazers. This formality then gave way to a more practical jersey along with a badge, sponsor's identification, shorts and socks. Traditionally the uniform was black, unless of course one of the competing teams was wearing a very dark coloured jersey in which case the referee would wear another colour to distinguish himself from both teams.

Television coverage has caused referee jerseys to be available in a number of colours. Mostly the colours are red, yellow, green, blue or black. Referees are required to wear black shorts, black socks and black boots.

They all carry a whistle, a watch (mostly two, one being used to determine time lost for stoppages), penalty cards, a data wallet with pen and paper, and of course a coin to determine which team has choice of end or kick-off.

The system of 'language-neutral' coloured cards for cautioning or dismissals originated with British referee, Ken Aston, who got the idea while sitting in his car at traffic lights. The first major use of penalty cards was in the 1970 FIFA World Cup but it was not until 1982 that they became mandatory. When cards were first introduced into the Scottish game, the Secretary of the SFA, Willie Allan, only issued yellow cards to referees as he felt that it was obvious when a referee ordered a player off the field of play... the player walked! However, he soon relented and the red card was introduced.

At the highest level, match officials use two-way radios to communicate with each other, and assistant referees may use electronic flags which signal to the referee when a button is pushed.

Refereeing Guidelines and The Laws of the Game as defined by FIFA

The laws of the game are controlled by the International Football Association Board (IFAB) of which the Scottish FA was a founding member in 1886.

The Powers and Duties of a Referee

- The Referee enforces the Laws of the Game.
- Controls the match in cooperation with the assistant referees and, where applicable, with the fourth official.
- Ensures that any ball used meets the requirements defined: i.e. spherical; made of leather or other suitable material; of a circumference of not more than 70 cm (28 ins) and not less than 68 cm (27 ins); not more than 450 g (16 oz) and not less than 410 g (14 oz) in weight at the start of the match; of a pressure equal to 8.5 lbs/sq to 15.6 lbs/sq in.
- Ensures that players' equipment meets the requirements defined: i.e. a player must not use equipment or wear anything that is dangerous to himself or another player (including any kind of jewellery); the basic compulsory equipment includes a jersey or shirt with sleeves – if undergarments are worn, the colour of the sleeve must be the same main colour as the sleeve of the jersey or shirt; shorts – if undershorts or tights are worn, they must be of the same main colour as the shorts; stockings – if tape or similar material is applied externally it must be the same colour as that part of the stocking it is applied to. Shin-guards and footwear must be worn. The footwear studs must have no rough or sharp edges which could cause injury to another player.

- Stops, suspends or abandons the match because of outside interference of any kind.
- Stops suspends or abandons the match, at his discretion, for any infringements of the Laws.
- Acts as timekeeper and keeps a record of the match.
- Stops the match if, in his opinion, a player is seriously injured and ensures that he is removed from the field of play. An injured player may only return to the field of play after the match has restarted.
- Allows play to continue until the ball is out of play if a player is, in his opinion, only slightly injured.
- Ensures that any player bleeding from a wound leaves the field of play. The player may only return on receiving a signal from the referee, who must be satisfied that the bleeding has stopped.
- Allows play to continue when the team against which an offence has been committed will benefit from such an advantage, and penalises the original offence if the anticipated advantage does not ensue at that time.
- Punishes the more serious offence when a player commits more than one offence at the same time.
- Takes disciplinary action against players of cautionable and sending-off offences. He is not obliged to take this action immediately but must do so when the ball next goes out of play.
- Takes action against officials who fail to conduct themselves in a responsible manner and may, at his discretion, expel them from the field of play and its immediate surrounds.
- Acts on the advice of the assistant referees regarding incidents that he has not seen.
- Ensures that no unauthorised persons enter the field of play.
- Indicates the restart of the match after it has been stopped.

- Provides the appropriate authorities with a match report, which includes information on any disciplinary action against players and/or team officials and any other incidents that occurred before, during or after the match.
- The decision of the referee regarding facts connected with play, including whether or not a goal is scored and the result of the match, are final.
- The referee may only change a decision on realising that it is incorrect or, at his discretion, on the advice of an assistant referee or the fourth official, provided that he has not restarted play or terminated the match.

Assistant Referees

Two assistant referees are appointed whose duties, subject to the decision of the referee, are to indicate:

- When the whole of the ball leaves the field of play.
- Which team is entitled to a corner kick, goal kick or throw-in.
- When a player may be penalised for being in an offside position.
- When a substitute is requested.
- When misconduct or any other incident occurs out of the view of the referee.
- When offences have been committed whenever the assistant referees have a better view than the referee (this includes offences committed in the penalty area).
- Whether, at penalty kicks, the goalkeeper moves off the goal line before the ball is kicked and if the ball crosses the line.

Offside

It is not an offence in itself to be in an offside position.

However a player **is** in an offside position if:

- He is nearer to his opponents' goal line than both the ball and the second-last opponent. I.E. any part of his head, body or feet is nearer his opponents' goal line than both the ball and the second last opponent (the last opponent normally being the goalkeeper).

A player is **not** in an offside position if:

- He is in his own half of the field of play.
- He is level with the second-last opponent.
- He is level with the last two opponents.
- He is level with or behind the ball.

In addition, there is no offside offence if a player receives the ball directly from a corner kick, a goal kick or a throw-in. An offside offence may occur if a player receives the ball directly from either a direct free kick or an indirect free kick if he is in an offside position at the moment the ball is kicked.

Cautionable Offences (Yellow Cards)

A player is cautioned and shown the yellow card if he commits any of the following offences: unsporting behaviour: dissent by word or action: persistent infringement of the Laws of the Game: delaying the restart of play: failure to respect the required distance when play is restarted with a corner kick, free kick or throw-in: entering or re-entering the field of play without the referee's permission: deliberately leaving the field of play without the referee's permission.

Sending-off Offences (Red Cards)

A player, substitute or substituted player is sent off if he commits any of the following offences: serious foul play; violent conduct; spitting at an opponent or any other person; denying the opposing team a goal or obvious goalscoring opportunity by deliberately handling the ball (this does not apply to a goalkeeper within his own penalty area); denying an obvious goalscoring opportunity to an opponent moving towards the player's goal by an offence punishable by a free kick or a penalty kick; using offensive, insulting or abusive language and/or gestures; receiving a second caution (yellow card) in the same match.

A player, substitute or substituted player who has been sent off must leave the vicinity of the field of play and the technical area.

Direct Free Kicks

A direct free kick is awarded to the opposing team if a player commits any of the following offences in a manner considered by the referee to be careless, reckless or using excessive force:

- Kicks or attempts to kick an opponent.
- Trips or attempts to trip an opponent.
- Jumps at an opponent.
- Charges an opponent.
- Strikes or attempts to strike an opponent.
- Pushes an opponent.
- Tackles an opponent.

A direct free kick is also awarded to the opposing team if a player commits any of the following offences:

- Holds an opponent.
- Spits at an opponent.
- Handles the ball deliberately (except for the goalkeeper within his own penalty area).

Note: A direct free kick is taken from the place where the offence occurred.

Penalty Kicks

A penalty kick is awarded if any of the ten Free Kick offences is committed by a player inside his own penalty area, irrespective of the position of the ball, provided it is in play.

The referee must confirm the following requirements before the penalty kick is taken:

- The kicker is identified.
- The ball is properly placed on the penalty mark.
- The goalkeeper is on the goal line between the goalposts and facing the kicker.
- The team-mates of the kicker and the goalkeeper are outside the penalty area, outside the penalty arc and behind the ball.

Feinting in the run-up to take a penalty kick to confuse opponents is permitted. However, feinting to kick the ball once the player has completed his run-up is considered an infringement of law 14 and an act of unsporting behaviour for which the player must be cautioned.

Indirect Free Kicks

An indirect free kick is awarded to the opposing team if a goalkeeper, inside his own penalty area, commits any of the following offences:

- Controls the ball with his hands for more than six seconds before releasing it from his possession.
- Touches the ball again with his hands after he has released it from his possession and before it has touched another player.
- Touches the ball with his hands after it has deliberately kicked to him by a team-mate.

- Touches the ball with his hands after he has received it directly from a throw-in taken by a team-mate.

An indirect free kick is also awarded to the opposing team if, in the opinion of the referee, a player:

- Plays in a dangerous manner.
- Impedes the progress of an opponent.
- Prevents the goalkeeper from releasing the ball from his hands.
- Commits any other offence fo which play is stopped to caution or send off a player.

The indirect free kick is taken from the place where the offence occurred.

Dimensions of the Pitch

Length: Minimum 60m (100 yards) – Maximum 120m (130 yards)

Width: Minimum 45m (50 yards) – Maximum 90m (100 yards)

The actual line must be the same width, which must not be more than 12cm (5 inches)

Dimensions of the Pitch for International Matches

Length: Minimum 100m (110 yards) – Maximum 110m (120 yards)

Width: Minimum 64m (70 yards) – Maximum 75m (80 yards)

The Goal Area

Two lines are drawn at right angles to the goal line, 5.5m (6 yards) from the inside of each goalpost. These lines extend into the field of play for a distance of 5.5m (6 yards) and are joined by a line drawn parallel with the goal line. The area bounded by these lines and the goal line is designated the goal area.

The Penalty Area

Two lines are drawn at right angles to the goal line, 16.5 metres (18 yards) from the inside of each goalpost. These lines extend into the field of play for a distance of 16.5 metres (18 yards) and are joined by a line drawn parallel with the goal line. The area bounded by these lines is designated the penalty area.

Within each penalty area, a penalty mark is made 11 metres (12 yards) from the midpoint between the goalposts and equidistant to them.

An arc of a circle with a radius of 9.15 metres (10 yards) from the centre of each penalty mark is drawn outside the penalty area. The purpose of this is to prevent players, particularly opposing players, encroaching into the penalty area or interfering with the run-up when the penalty kick is being taken.

If a penalty kick has to be taken or retaken, the duration of either half is extended until the penalty is completed.

Flagposts

A flagpost, not less than 1.5 metre (5 feet), with a non-pointed top and a flag must be placed at each corner.

A quarter circle with a radius of 1 metre (1 yard) from each corner flagpost is drawn inside the field of play.

Flagposts may also be placed at each end of the half-way line, not less than 1 metre (1 yard) outside the touchline.

Goals

The distance between the posts is 7.32 metres (8 yards) and the distance from the lower edge of the crossbar to the ground is 2.44 metres (8 feet).

A goal is scored when the whole of the ball passes over the goal line, between the goalposts and under the crossbar, provided that no infringement of the Laws of the Game has been committed by the team scoring the goal.

Substitutes

In all matches the names of the substitutes must be given to the referee prior to the start of the match along with the team sheet. Any substitute whose name is not given to the referee at this time may not take part in the match.

To replace a player with a substitute, the following conditions must be observed.

- The referee must be informed before any proposed substitution is made.
- The substitute only enters the field of play after the player being replaced has left and after receiving a signal from the referee.
- The substitute only enters the field of play at the halfway line and during a stoppage in the match.
- The substitution is completed when a substitute becomes a player and the player he has replaced becomes a substituted player.
- The substituted player takes no further part in the match.
- All substitutes are subject to the authority and jurisdiction of the referee, whether called upon to play or not.
- Any of the other players may change places with the goalkeeper provided the referee is informed before the change is made, and the change is made during a stoppage in the match.

'Then strip, lad and to it though cold be the weather, and if by mischance you should happen to fall,

there are worse things in life than a tumble on heather,

for life is itself but a game at football.'

On the lifting of the Banner of the House of Buccleuch.
Sir Walter Scott 1815

'Ah finally went tae Specsavers and they said ah've even got eyes at the back o' ma heid!'

Archibald B. 'Big Erchie' Smith, 2013

Luath Press Limited
committed to publishing well written books worth reading

LUATH PRESS takes its name from Robert Burns, whose little collie Luath (*Gael.*, swift or nimble) tripped up Jean Armour at a wedding and gave him the chance to speak to the woman who was to be his wife and the abiding love of his life. Burns called one of 'The Twa Dogs' Luath after Cuchullin's hunting dog in Ossian's *Fingal*. Luath Press was established in 1981 in the heart of Burns country, and now resides a few steps up the road from Burns' first lodgings on Edinburgh's Royal Mile.

Luath offers you distinctive writing with a hint of unexpected pleasures.

Most bookshops in the UK, the US, Canada, Australia, New Zealand and parts of Europe either carry our books in stock or can order them for you. To order direct from us, please send a £sterling cheque, postal order, international money order or your credit card details (number, address of cardholder and expiry date) to us at the address below. Please add post and packing as follows: UK – £1.00 per delivery address; overseas surface mail – £2.50 per delivery address; overseas airmail – £3.50 for the first book to each delivery address, plus £1.00 for each additional book by airmail to the same address. If your order is a gift, we will happily enclose your card or message at no extra charge.

Luath Press Limited
543/2 Castlehill
The Royal Mile
Edinburgh EH1 2ND
Scotland
Telephone: 0131 225 4326 (24 hours)
Fax: 0131 225 4324
email: sales@luath.co.uk
Website: www.luath.co.uk

ILLUSTRATION: IAN KELLAS